AF378807

THE PRIVATE WORLD
OF LEROY BROWN

Also by Rhodri Jones and published by Dent:
Delroy is Here
(nominated for the 1983 Carnegie Medal)
A Fine Mess You've Got Us Into!
A Collection of Comic Disasters
Compiled by Rhodri Jones and
illustrated by Tony Kerins

The Private World of Leroy Brown

Rhodri Jones

Illustrated by Caroline Binch

J.M. Dent & Sons Ltd
London & Melbourne

First published 1987
© Rhodri Jones 1987
Illustrations © J.M. Dent & Sons Ltd 1987

Typeset in 11½/13½ pt Baskerville
by Inforum Ltd, Portsmouth
Made in Great Britain
by Biddles Ltd, Guildford, Surrey
for J.M. Dent & Sons Ltd
Aldine House, 33 Welbeck Street, London W1M 8LX

British Library Cataloguing in Publication Data

Jones, Rhodri
  The private world of Leroy Brown.
  I. Title
  823'.914[J]   PZ7
  ISBN 0–460–06260–3

Contents

Leroy's First Day

Leroy couldn't sleep. Next morning was his first day at the big school. And he was scared.

Earlier that evening, his older brother Floyd had told him all about it.

'You know it call Colditz, don' you? The teachers is hard, man, like prison guards. You can' do not'in wit'out they comes down on you like a ton o' bricks. They got rules 'bout everyt'in'.'

Leroy went tense, but he tried not to show it.

'You wanna watch Mr Garfield,' Floyd continued. ''E the worse o' the lot. 'E the deputy 'ead. 'E vicious, man. Squeak an' 'e give you lines.'

Floyd waited and watched for some reaction. But Leroy didn't blink.

'An' you gets 'omework, you know. You can' call you' time you' own. An' if you don' do it, you geta a detention.'

Floyd waited and watched again. But Leroy stared him out.

'They got all kind o' punishment. Lines, detention, suspension. They don' use the cane no more.' He sounded disappointed. Then he had a sudden spurt of inspiration. 'But if you real bad, they makes you 'ang from the wall bars in the gym fo' two hours.'

'Floyd!' warned Mum in a thunderous voice, glaring at him.

'I were only kiddin',' Floyd protested.

But was he? There was a mischievous smile playing round his eyes and lips.

Leroy sucked his teeth slowly and contemptuously. 'I ain't worried,' he said. Or was he?

After a while, Floyd began again.

'They does t'ings to new boys,' he said. 'They 'as these 'nitiations.' He waited to make sure he had Leroy's attention. 'Like grabbin' you by the arms an' legs an' givin' you bumps.'

Leroy eyed his brother warily.

'Like taxin' you. Takin' all you' books an' not lettin' you 'ave 'em back till you've paid for 'em.'

Leroy took that without flinching.

Floyd racked his brains for another example.

'Yeah,' he cried triumphantly. 'Like shovin' you' 'ead down the loo an' pullin' the chain.'

'Floyd!' Mum shouted. There was danger in her voice. 'What you doin' fillin' 'is 'ead wit' t'ings like that? You gonna give 'im nightmares.'

'It were only a bit o' fun,' Floyd retorted, though not very convincingly.

But was it? There was still a smile hovering over Floyd's face and pulling at his mouth.

Leroy casually stretched his arms and arched his back and yawned. 'I ain't worried,' he said.

But he was. Now, in bed, he couldn't sleep. Everything Floyd had told him came crowding back to haunt him. Was it really going to be like that?

Floyd's snores from the other bed didn't help either. It was all right for him.

At some point in the restless night came the muffled sounds of someone grumbling and stumbling about. Dad was getting ready for the early shift.

And then in no time at all the door of the bedroom was pushed open and Mum was there to wake him.

'Now you make sure you washes you' face right,' she told him. 'An' don' forget you' ears.'

She turned and shook Floyd's shoulder.

'Come on, you,' she said. 'You don' wanna be late on you' first day back.'

Floyd grunted and pulled the sheet up over his head.

When Leroy went into the kitchen, Paulette was already

sitting at the table eating her cornflakes.

'Ooh!' she cried, her face all lit up. 'Don' 'e look nice in 'is uniform.'

Leroy gave her a cold stare.

Mum glanced round to inspect him. ''E'll do.'

'I wish I 'ad a uniform like that,' Paulette moaned.

'You will,' said Mum ominously. 'You will.'

Mum had to call Floyd three times before he finally appeared, his eyes still full of sleep.

'You sure you wash?' Mum asked suspiciously.

'Yeah,' Floyd mumbled. 'Course I 'as.'

He stumbled to the table and sat down. Then his eyes cleared and he looked across at Leroy.

'Oh yeah, I forgets,' he said. 'An' they 'olds you upside down an' shakes you till all you' money drop out, an' then they takes it.'

'Floyd!' Mum roared, rounding on him.

Floyd ducked his head and reached for the cornflakes packet.

Leroy took a bite of his toast and chewed it slowly, round and round. He brooded on what Floyd had said and on the day ahead. He wasn't looking forward to it.

When it was time to go, Mum said to Floyd, 'You gonna take 'im up, ain't you?'

Floyd protested. 'Aw, Mum! What my mates gonna t'ink? 'Oldin' my kid brother by the 'and. That too shamin'.'

'Just the first day,' Mum coaxed.

But Floyd was already out of the door.

'Drat that boy,' Mum cried. 'I don' know what get into 'im these days. An' 'e ain't even finish 'is breakfast.'

She gave a deep sigh. 'I 'spects I'll 'ave to do it myself. As usual.'

Leroy was suddenly alarmed. He had his mates too. And his pride.

'But Mum,' he began. 'I don' need . . .'

'Now don' you start,' Mum warned. 'I ain't lettin' you go up there on you' own. Not on you' first day.'

'But . . .' Leroy tried again.

'An' that's that,' said Mum finally.

Leroy had to put up with it. But he went on worrying.

'Come on, Mum,' Paulette cried, dancing from one foot to another. She seemed to be excited about going back to school. But then she was only eight.

Mum struggled into her coat. She pushed Leroy and Paulette out of the door in front of her and double locked it behind her.

'I 'opes no one break in,' she said.

There had been a spate of burglaries recently on the estate.

They set off along the walkway in the direction of the lift.

As luck would have it, at that moment Mrs Macauley came shuffling towards them. She was one of their neighbours. She'd been to get her newspaper.

Mrs Macauley smiled at them and then beamed at Leroy.

'Don' 'e look smart!' she exclaimed. 'All doll up in 'is new uniform.'

Leroy tried hard not to scowl.

'Yeah,' said Mum. 'It 'is first day at the big school.'

Leroy couldn't imagine why she sounded so proud. He was the one going there, not her. And he didn't feel proud. Just scared.

' 'E sure is gettin' to be a big man,' glowed Mrs Macauley.

Leroy was glad when Mum moved on.

Mrs Macauley called after them. 'Ain't no use tryin' the lift. It broke again.'

They began to trudge down the five flights of stairs. There was the usual smell of stale dustbins and cats' pee.

Leroy worried about what Mrs Macauley had said about his uniform. It was the first time he had worn it in public. And he was carrying a shiny new brief-case as well. He didn't feel comfortable. His tie was strangling him. His shoes wouldn't bend properly when he walked. And the sleeves of his blazer kept falling down and swallowing his hands. He'd told Mum in the shop it was too big, but she wouldn't listen. All she'd said was, 'You's a growin' boy.' As if his arms were going to stretch four inches!

Floyd didn't have to wear uniform. At least that was what he said. How come he got away with it? It wasn't right.

When they reached the main road, Mum glanced up and down. 'No point in waitin' fo' a bus,' she said.

It showed a sad lack of faith in London Transport, Leroy thought. Especially since Dad was a bus-driver. But then perhaps she had inside knowledge.

Not that they had far to go – down to the shopping centre, and then up the avenue.

Paulette's school was first. It had been Leroy's school too until six weeks ago.

Mr Duffy, the headmaster, was in the playground.

'Good morning, Mrs Brown,' he cried. 'Hello, Paulette. Nice to be back? And Leroy. Looking forward to the big school? Doesn't he look smart? And he's grown, hasn't he?'

Leroy quite liked Mr Duffy. There was just one thing. He couldn't stop talking.

'I was sorry to see him leave. Best footballer we ever had. To watch him trap the ball and dribble down the field and shoot for goal was a joy. An absolute joy. Never mind, I've no doubt he'll do great things at the big school. He'll be a credit to us all. The secondary schools think they do all the work, but where would they be without us? Eh? We lay the foundations. We set the standards. We . . .'

Mum was beginning to look strained. Paulette had already run off to join her friends.

'We better be goin',' Mum managed to get in when Mr Duffy eventually paused for breath.

'Of course,' said Mr Duffy. 'Don't want to be late on our first day, now do we? Good luck, Leroy.'

As they turned to go, they heard Mr Duffy cry, 'Ah, Mr Jackson, good morning . . .'

Beechcroft High School was further along the avenue. A curving drive led from the wide entrance gates up to the school itself. Already, a procession of pupils and teachers was grinding its way along it. Leroy and his Mum tagged on at the end.

Leroy knew he was big for his age. He couldn't very well forget it the way everyone kept reminding him. But most of the boys and girls around him looked even bigger. He'd seen a lot of them before, of course, when they'd come pouring out of school and down the avenue past Beechcroft Junior. But close to, they somehow looked enormous, even to him.

Then the building came into sight. It was colossal! Three storeys high, spreading out wide, all glass. Leroy wondered how he would ever find his way about. He was bound to get lost. As he neared the school, he kept his eyes peeled for familiar faces. Calamity was going to be there, and Veronica Wright and Angie and Lalji – quite a few of the pupils from Beechcroft Junior, in fact.

A lot of parents had chosen other schools further away, because they too had seen the pupils from Beechcroft High swarming out at four o'clock, pushing, fighting and swearing. They said they didn't want their children to go to a school like that.

Rounding the corner to the main entrance, Leroy worried about what Calamity and the others would say when they saw that Mum had brought him. He'd never live it down.

But it was all right. There were other parents there, standing about with their children, waiting for school to begin. And there was Calamity, his fair hair sticking up all over his head. He had the kind of hair that always stood up no matter how much he combed it or tried to plaster it down.

His mum was with him as well. And Veronica Wright was there, too, with her mum.

'Hi,' Leroy said to Calamity.

'Hi,' Calamity said back. He gave a sickly grin before sinking back into a gloomy stupor.

That was strange. Usually, Calamity was full of jokes and chat. You couldn't stop him.

Perhaps it was because his mum was there. Or was he

nervous, too? Leroy began to feel better.

While the mothers talked, Leroy glanced round the other children waiting. They were quiet as well, with miserable-looking faces and fearful expressions – like early Christians in one of Mr Duffy's stories, about to be thrown to the lions.

Leroy gulped. All the things Floyd had said about the school came rushing back to him. The boys playing a mad game of football on the ground certainly did look big. Somehow he didn't mind so much now about Mum coming.

The honking of a hooter made him jump. It went on and on like a demented cow. The main doors opened and a man came out. He was wrapped in a black sort of cloak, which he was flapping about. He looked like a bat. In a minute, he'd be taking off.

'That's called a gown,' Veronica Wright said, loud enough for everyone to hear.

Trust her to know.

'Come along,' the man was calling out in an impatient voice. 'All new pupils this way.'

'It's Mr Garfield,' Calamity whispered to Leroy. ''E's the deputy 'ead.'

''Ow you know?' Leroy demanded.

'I seen 'im in the street once,' Calamity told him. 'When I was with my brother. My brother says 'e's fierce.'

So this was the dreaded Mr Garfield Floyd talked about. Leroy examined him carefully. He had a domed bald head surrounded by a fringe of grey hair. His face was dry and cracked. He had a bristly grey moustache and wild bushy grey eyebrows. He looked fierce all right.

Mums and dads were saying their goodbyes. The children were drifting towards the door.

'Don' forget to collect Paulette,' Mum reminded Leroy.

'Yeah, Mum.'

For one horrified moment, Leroy thought she was going to kiss him, but she just touched him on the arm and said, 'You be good, you 'ear?'

'Yeah, Mum.'

He pulled himself up to his full height and marched boldly up to the entrance. He wasn't afraid. He'd show them. He was sure Mum was watching, but he didn't look back.

In the hall, teachers were bustling about getting the pupils into some kind of order. Leroy was grabbed, pushed into line and told to sit on the floor.

Mr Garfield was standing in the middle of the stage in front of them, arms folded, mouth grimly shut, eyes drilling along row after row. No one dared utter a sound.

They sat like that for five minutes.

Then there was some kind of disturbance at the door and the clip-clop of heels advancing across the wooden floor.

Leroy carefully swung his head round to see who it was. So did everyone else. A woman was swooping down on them. She had a broad smile on her face. She was wearing a black gown like Mr Garfield's. It flew out behind her.

'Stand up,' Mr Garfield roared at them.

Leroy struggled to his feet with the rest of them.

The woman climbed up the stairs at the side of the stage and joined Mr Garfield in the centre. She began waving her arms at them.

'Sit down,' Mr Garfield roared.

They sank to the floor again, shuffling and elbowing each other to make room for themselves.

While the woman waited for order to be restored, Mr Garfield fixed his eye on something interesting on the ceiling above him. Leroy couldn't work out what it was.

'Good morning, children,' the woman said, smiling at them.

There was no response.

The woman frowned her disappointment.

'That's not a very good start, is it?' she cried brightly. 'It's the custom in this school when I say "Good morning, children" for you to answer. Let's try it again, shall we?'

She cleared her throat. 'Good morning, children.'

'Good morning, miss,' came a ragged mumble.

The woman hesitated for a moment and then decided to

accept it as the best she was likely to get.

'I am Mrs Worthington,' she announced. 'I am your headmistress.'

She waited, eyes darting from pupil to pupil, to make sure the information had sunk in.

When she was confident that it had, she went on, 'I am very pleased to welcome you here this morning as new pupils of Beechcroft High School. I am sure you are going to be happy and successful here. You are coming to a very good school. Your parents couldn't have made a better choice for you. We . . .'

Mrs Worthington was like Mr Duffy, Leroy decided. She couldn't stop talking. She went on and on.

'. . . magnificent opportunities . . . splendid facilities . . . outstanding achievements . . . first-class staff . . . enviable record . . .'

But at last she drew to a close. 'And now I hand you over to my deputy, Mr Garfield, who will induct you into the rest of the proceedings.'

It sounded painful to Leroy.

Mr Garfield drew his startled gaze down from the ceiling. There was a quiet but heated exchange between him and Mrs Worthington. Leroy was near enough to hear her hiss, 'I've got a parent waiting.' Mr Garfield closed his mouth like a trap.

Mrs Worthington turned to the pupils and with a wide smile said, 'Good morning, children.'

She waited just long enough to make sure a rumbling 'Good morning, miss' was on its way back to her before charging down the steps off the stage and out of the hall.

Mr Garfield's eyes followed venomously. Then he focused on the pupils in front of him.

'Sit up straight,' he barked. A shiver ran through them and they shot up like soldiers on parade.

'Now listen,' he went on grimly, 'and listen carefully because I'm not going to repeat myself.' He raked them with a steely stare. 'We have discipline in this school. We have rules. And if you break them, then heaven help you.'

He paused long enough to let that sink in. Then he launched into a long explanation of what the rules were. By the end of it, he was sweating and the pupils were thoroughly confused. Leroy couldn't remember half of what he had said.

But it seemed to have done Mr Garfield some good. Having delivered his lecture he calmed down.

'Now let's get you sorted into your forms,' he said in a voice that was almost pleasant. 'We'll start with 1B. When I call out your names, go and stand on the side. Mr Baxter, will you come and see they get it right, please?'

The teacher who stepped forward was tall and thin. He was wearing gold-rimmed spectacles that gave his face a rather worried look.

Leroy heard his name being called out and went to join the slowly gathering crowd round Mr Baxter. Next came Calamity and later Veronica Wright.

When the class appeared to be complete, Mr Garfield cried, 'That's your lot, Mr Baxter. Take them away.'

The teacher led them out of the hall, up the stairs and into a classroom.

'Find yourselves seats,' Mr Baxter said. 'Anywhere will do for the moment. We'll sort you out later.'

In his classroom, Mr Baxter seemed to be slightly more confident.

Quickly and quietly, the pupils settled themselves. Leroy and Calamity made sure they were sitting next to each other. Everyone waited expectantly for Mr Baxter to begin.

'First of all,' he said, 'I'm going to call out your names, and I want each of you to stand up when your name is called. That way I can get to know you, and you can get to know each other.'

He consulted a sheet of paper.

'Angela Allcock . . . Lalji Bhandari . . . Leroy Brown . . . Jane Bryon . . .'

As Leroy stood up, Mr Baxter's eyes widened.

'You *are* big for a first former, aren't you?' he said in awed tones. He looked as though he couldn't quite believe what he was seeing.

Well, it's not my fault, Leroy wanted to say. But he didn't.

'Terence Callum . . . Teresa Collins . . . Maria Costa . . .'

When he had finished the roll call, Mr Baxter handed out the school rules. There were two sheets of them, closely typed. They went from one to ninety-two. They were about uniform, punctuality, behaviour inside school, in the playground and even outside school. They had a rule for everything.

'The first thing you've got to do tonight when you get home,' Mr Baxter told them, 'is to sit down and learn them off by heart.'

Leroy groaned. Mr Garfield. Rules. Homework. Colditz. It looked as though Floyd had been right.

It was a relief when the hooter suddenly erupted for break.

'Let's 'ave a game o' football,' Calamity suggested.

Leroy cheered up. 'Yeah.'

According to the rules, the first year had to use the top playground. They made their way up the steps.

But when they arrived, they found the older boys had already taken it over. They were racing madly up and down after a football, hacking at each other, jumping on each other's backs, whirling in the air with Kung Fu kicks.

Veronica had followed Leroy and Calamity up the steps with her friend Angie. She gazed indignantly at the rampaging footballers.

'They ain't supposed to be 'ere,' she cried. 'This is supposed to be our playground. Like Mr Baxter said.'

She gave a further gasp of annoyance. 'And they got a football. They ain't supposed to play with anythin' bigger than a tennis ball. It's Rule 25.'

Leroy and Calamity stared at the scene despondently for a while and then at each other. There was no way they were going to be able to play football there. Not unless they wanted a broken arm or a cracked head. They sighed and went to stand by the wire fence that separated the school grounds from the gardens of adjoining houses. Groups of other boys and girls strolled past them, chatting and laughing. Some of them eyed Leroy and Calamity curiously. Leroy kept on the alert.

'You gotta watch out,' he told Calamity. 'They got 'nitiations. Floyd tell me.'

Calamity looked blank. 'What's them?'

'T'ings they does to you when you new. Like givin' you bumps. Or taxin' you. Or t'iefin' you' money. Or . . .'

He didn't like to mention what they did in the toilets. He would have to go there sometime before the end of break.

'Yeah,' said Calamity. 'I 'ear that too.'

Anxiously, he scanned the area round them for a possible attack. Leroy spotted Floyd in the distance with a friend. They were coming towards them.

'Hi,' Floyd said sourly.

His friend stopped to look. 'That you' brother?' he asked.

'Yeah,' said Floyd as if admitting to something shameful.

The friend started to laugh with delight. 'Man, 'e bigger than what you are.'

'Oh yeah?' said Floyd. He didn't seem to think it was funny.

Neither did Leroy. He was getting tired of hearing comments about his size.

The friend asked, 'What d'you t'ink o' it so far?'

'Not much,' Leroy replied.

'You wait,' said Floyd. 'It get worse.'

There was a blast of a whistle. The footballers froze and then made a mad scramble to get clear. Mr Garfield came storming up the steps to the top playground.

'Get off, you louts!' he screamed. 'This isn't your playground! It's for the first and second years!'

His bushy eyebrows were raised high on his forehead. It looked as though his domed head was going to erupt like a volcano.

He went careering round the playground, searching for someone to pounce on. But all the footballers had dis-

appeared. So had Floyd's friend, Leroy noticed. And then, Mr Garfield was raging in front of them.

'What are you doing here, Brown?' he demanded.

Leroy jumped, but it was his brother who answered. 'Not'in, sir.'

Floyd was suddenly looking worried.

'Nothing?' Mr Garfield roared. 'What d'you mean "Nothing"? Don't you know this playground is out of bounds to fourth formers?'

'Yes, sir.'

'Then get off it!'

'Sorry, sir,' Floyd said, and he began to move.

'Wait!' shrieked Mr Garfield.

Floyd stopped dead in his tracks and slowly swung round. He waited apprehensively for the next words.

'What d'you call that you're wearing?' Mr Garfield demanded.

Floyd looked down at his flowered shirt, his jeans and his trainers.

'What, sir?' he asked, trying to appear innocent.

'That's not school uniform.'

Floyd swallowed and gave up the struggle. 'No, sir,' he mumbled. Leroy was astounded. He had never heard his brother sound so humble.

Mr Garfield gave an exasperated snort. 'I've never known anyone like you. You're useless. What are you?'

'I'm useless, sir,' Floyd meekly agreed.

'Report to me first thing tomorrow morning,' Mr Garfield snapped. 'And I want to see you in full school uniform. Blazer. Tie. Shirt – white, grey or light blue. Trousers – grey. Shoes – black. Is that clear?'

'Yes, sir,' Floyd muttered. He turned and walked away. His whole body was drooping. He looked as though he'd shrunk six inches.

Mr Garfield cast a baleful eye on Leroy and Calamity and then stalked back into the middle of the playground to see who else he could catch.

'Wow!' breathed Calamity who had been watching the whole scene spellbound. 'Mr Garfield sure is fierce.'

'Yeah,' agreed Leroy. 'That what my brother tell me.'

He smiled. It was the first time he'd smiled all day.

The hooter honked for the end of break.

'I gotta go to the lav,' Leroy cried.

'Me too,' said Calamity.

They rushed down to the main entrance. It was only when they reached it that they realized they didn't know where the boys' lavatories were.

They asked a teacher who appeared to be on duty.

'But you can't go now,' the teacher said. 'Break's finished.'

'But, sir!' Leroy protested.

'Oh, very well,' the teacher relented, and he pointed them in the right direction.

There were other boys there, but Leroy was relieved to discover they had more urgent business on their minds than initiations.

They were late getting back to their form room. Mr Baxter gave them a dirty look before beginning to dictate their timetables.

He went at a tremendous lick. Leroy had a hard job of it to keep up with the relentless list of subjects, teachers and rooms.

'What's environmental studies?' Calamity whispered halfway through.

Leroy scowled at him. 'Don' you know not'in'?' He'd been puzzling over what it meant himself.

Next, Mr Baxter took them on a tour of the school.

It was vast. There were so many things Leroy had never seen before. He gawped at the science labs, the technical workshops, the art studios, the gymnasiums.

Compared with his junior school, there was so much equipment. He was dying to use it all. Take the gyms. They had basketball stands, trampolines, weights, horses, table-tennis tables.

He didn't like the look of the wall-bars, though.

By the end of the tour, he was exhausted and bewildered. It would be so easy to get lost.

'It sure is big,' Calamity murmured, awe-struck. 'I ain't never gonna find my way round.'

'Huh!' cried Leroy. 'Ain't not'in' to it.'

Luckily, the dining room was one of the easier places to find.

Leroy felt better after sausages, beans and chips, followed by jam-roll and custard. At least the meals were the same.

The big boys had taken over the top playground again. All Leroy and Calamity could do was stand around and look on.

Leroy watched glumly as a boy was kicked to the ground and everyone else piled on top of him.

'Look out,' Calamity warned. ''Ere's Mr Garfield.'

The deputy head was slowly mounting the steps to the top playground. The footballers hadn't noticed him yet. Leroy wondered if he should let them know. They were bound to get into trouble. Mr Garfield would go spare.

But the deputy head just stood there. He appeared to be following the game with interest. Something had happened to his face. It was relaxed and smiling.

Leroy couldn't make it out. It was against the rules for senior boys to play on the top playground. And with a football too. Why wasn't Mr Garfield doing anything about it?

Some of the footballers had seen him by now. They stumbled and broke off their play. One of them scooped up the ball and hid it behind his back. They went into a huddle. When they separated, the boy who had picked up the ball strolled away empty-handed. One of the others must have taken the ball and was secreting it away to safety. Slowly they all drifted away.

Mr Garfield was watching all this, and yet he didn't seem to notice anything. He just went on smiling and nodding his head pleasantly. Leroy couldn't understand it.

Then Mr Garfield caught sight of Leroy and Calamity.

Leroy stiffened and gave Calamity a nudge. It looked as though Mr Garfield was coming towards them.

'Ah,' the deputy head cried. 'How are you first formers settling in?' His voice was jovial and friendly.

'All right,' Leroy answered guardedly.

'It'll seem a bit strange to start with, but you'll soon get used to it,' Mr Garfield went on. He beamed down at them like Santa Claus.

Then he said to Leroy, 'You're big for your age, aren't you?'

Leroy didn't dare say anything.

Mr Garfield was taking a closer look at him, bending towards him and half closing his eyes. Leroy could see every single hair sprouting up and twirling round in those bushy eyebrows. He stayed absolutely still.

'I know that face,' Mr Garfield said. 'What's your name?'

Leroy told him.

'Of course,' Mr Garfield exclaimed. 'You've got a brother here, haven't you? Floyd.'

'Yes, sir.'

'I was sure I knew the face,' Mr Garfield cried triumphantly. 'Well, Floyd's not a bad lad. Oh, he can be a bit of a rascal, but he's all right. If you turn out like him, you won't be doing too badly.'

He gave Leroy a playful jab on the arm and chuckled.

Leroy couldn't believe what he was hearing and seeing. Only a few hours before, Mr Garfield had been calling Floyd every name under the sun. And now here he was, talking about him like a jolly uncle.

'Yes, he's not a bad lad,' the deputy head said again, and he wandered off as if he was in a world of his own, his hands behind his back twirling the loose sleeves of his gown round and round.

'I thought Mr Garfield was supposed to be fierce,' said Calamity.

'Well, 'e were this mornin',' said Leroy. 'You seen 'im.'

'Yeah,' agreed Calamity. ''E sure lay into your brother.'

It was a mystery all right.

When the hooter summoned them back for the afternoon session, 1B had to go to Room 19 for French. Real lessons were beginning. Leroy and Calamity and the others went along corridors and up stairs trying to find the room. They didn't like to ask any of the teachers or the bigger boys and girls who pushed past them.

Then Veronica Wright appeared.

'I know where it is,' she said smugly.

She led them straight to Room 19 where Mrs Curry was waiting for them.

Then it was English in Room 6 with Mr Delgado.

Mrs Curry and Mr Delgado both gave them long lectures on how important their particular subjects were. The way they talked you'd think there weren't any other subjects. They both issued the class with text books and exercise books. By the end of the afternoon, Leroy's case was almost full.

But at last the hooter went to announce their release, and they were free.

'They don't 'alf pile on the 'omework,' Calamity complained as he and Leroy made their way down the drive.

'Yeah,' agreed Leroy. 'Them rules to learn. An' French. An' English.' He sucked his teeth in disgust. 'An' it just the first day.'

'You gonna do it?' Calamity asked.

Leroy gave him a cautious look. 'I t'inks 'bout it,' he said, without committing himself.

'Yeah, well,' said Calamity. 'I'll think about it too.'

They separated at the school gates. Calamity lived in a different direction from Leroy, down by the railway.

'See you then,' he said.

'Yeah, tomorrow,' Leroy replied.

As he walked down the avenue to Beechcroft Junior School to pick up Paulette, Leroy brooded over the day. Floyd had been right about some things. All those rules. All that homework. But what about the funny way Mr Garfield had carried on? And what about those initiations Floyd talked about? There hadn't been any sign of them.

He was so lost in thought that he didn't realize at first that there was someone standing in his path blocking his way.

'You got 50p?'

Leroy squinted up at the speaker. He was a black boy. He was about the same age as Floyd. Leroy wasn't sure if he was a pupil at the school or not. He wasn't wearing uniform.

'Ain't got 50p,' Leroy told him and made to move on.

But the boy wouldn't let him pass. He grabbed Leroy by the arm and held on hard. It hurt.

'I wants 50p,' he hissed. His face was screwed up and dangerous.

'Get off,' Leroy cried. 'I ain't 'ave no money.' He struck at the boy's arm with his hand to try to break his hold.

The boy let go and seized the lapels of Leroy's blazer instead. He crushed them in his fists and yanked Leroy up on his toes. Leroy was big, but this boy was bigger.

'You gives me you' money,' the boy snarled, 'or I shakes it out you.'

Leroy breathed fiercely into the boy's face and stared enraged into his eyes. It was then that the thought came to him. Was this an initiation? Was this what it was like?

Then he was seething with yet more anger. No, it wasn't. This was no initiation. It was plain downright extortion. And he wasn't having it.

He went into furious action. He swung his case round again and again to whack the boy in the back. With the palm of his other hand he pushed the boy's face back with all his strength. He jerked from side to side to weaken the boy's hold on his blazer. The boy hung on, but it was clear from the boy's startled eyes that he was taken by surprise.

Suddenly, Floyd was there. He had his arm round the boy's neck and was dragging him away. Leroy was free.

'What you doin' to my brother?' Floyd was yelling. Leroy had never heard him sound so angry.

The boy was struggling to keep his balance. His fingers

grappled with Floyd's arm to prevent himself from being strangled. His eyes were twisting round wildly in his head, trying to see who was attacking him.

Floyd deposited him on the pavement.

The boy scrambled round ready to leap up. But then he saw who it was. He relaxed. He slowly got to his feet and stood there dusting off his hands and the seat of his jeans.

'I didn' know 'e were you' brother, Floyd,' he said. He looked quite sheepish.

'Well, you knows now, Earl,' Floyd told him.

'I were only axin' 'im fo' a loan.'

Floyd sucked his teeth with contempt. 'Cha! I knows you' loans. Don' you ax 'im again.'

'OK, man, OK.'

Earl turned to Leroy and stuck out his hand.

'No 'ard feelin's?'

There wasn't much else Leroy could do but shake Earl's hand.

Earl looked about him uncertainly as though trying to decide where to go next. He took a few steps and then stopped.

'Don' suppose you can loan me 50p?' he asked Floyd.

'Naw!' Floyd yelled at him.

Earl shrugged his shoulders and strolled on down the avenue.

'You all right?' Floyd asked Leroy.

'Sure,' Leroy retorted. 'I were just gettin' on top o' 'im when you come along.'

'You gotta watch you'self,' Floyd went on. 'There's lots o' guys like Earl around. 'E ain't that bad. 'E just like to take advantage when 'e can. 'E ain't very bright, though. You can tell. Fancy pickin' on somebody you' size. Still. You've gotta remember to stand up fo' you'self.'

Leroy was indignant. 'That's what I were doin'.'

But Floyd didn't seem to take the point.

'Come on,' he said. 'Let's go collect Paulette.'

Floyd didn't usually bother. He left that kind of thing to

Leroy. Walking beside his brother, Leroy wondered if Floyd was doing it to make sure no one else molested him. To protect him from any further attacks.

Not that he needed any protection. He could look after himself. Not that he minded Floyd's company either. Perhaps Floyd wasn't so bad after all. Wasn't that what Mr Garfield had said?

''Ere,' Leroy cried, 'I t'ought you told me Mr Garfield were fierce.'

'Yeah, well 'e is,' said Floyd. Didn' you see the way 'e go at me this mornin'? 'Bout my uniform?'

'Yeah, but 'e were different later on,' Leroy said, and told Floyd about his meeting with Mr Garfield. ''E were real nice to me.'

'When were that?' Floyd asked.

''Bout the end o' lunch break.'

'Aw,' Floyd exclaimed, 'that explain it. I 'as Mr Garfield fo' religious studies. 'E a kind o' Jekyll an' 'Yde character. When I 'as 'im in the mornin', 'e bite you' 'ead off an' 'e real mean. But when I 'as 'im in the afternoon, 'e quite different. 'E sort o' mellow an' easy-goin'. Like 'e floatin' on air. But even so, nobody like to get too close to 'im.'

'Why not?' Leroy asked.

''Cause 'e stink like a distillery.'

Funny, Leroy thought. Drink didn't affect Dad that way. When he had too much rum at Christmas, it had the opposite effect. It gave him a sore head and made him growl.

Still, it was fascinating what Floyd had told him. Leroy stayed fascinated as Floyd went on to tell him about all the other teachers.

When they reached home, Paulette rushed straight into the kitchen.

'Mum, Mum,' she cried. 'Pete's 'ad babies.'

Mum turned a sceptical eye on her. ''Ow can 'e 'ave babies if 'e call Pete?'

'I dunno,' said Paulette.

Leroy and Floyd exchanged glances. Paulette had

wearied them all the way home with her account of the achievements of the class hamster.

'My,' exclaimed Mum, catching sight of Floyd. 'You's 'ome early. What get into you? We's usually still waitin' at bed-time fo' you to show up.'

'Can' I come straight 'ome from school fo' once?' Floyd demanded.

'Sure, sure,' Mum said soothingly. 'I ain't sayin' I ain't pleased to see you.'

She eyed Leroy thoughtfully. ''Ow were school?' she asked at last.

'It were OK,' Leroy told her. 'I soon gets it lick into shape,' he added casually.

Mum went on watching him, her eyes getting larger and her mouth tightening in the effort to control her amusement. But it was no use. Her body began to shake. Her face creased up and she burst out laughing.

Leroy examined her coolly for a moment. Then he decided he didn't mind. He even felt his own lips begin to twitch. If he wasn't careful, he'd be laughing too.

Calamity's Idea

Calamity had an idea.

Immediately, alarm bells began to jangle in Leroy's head. Terence Callum wasn't called Calamity for nothing. He was a real bungler. Everything he touched became a catastrophe. A walking disaster-area, that was Calamity.

They were strolling down the drive after school. On their right was a wide grass verge with a few spindly trees. They hadn't stood much chance with the hordes of pupils that poured up and down the drive daily. Some of them had trailing branches, others had been snapped in half, leaving lifeless stumps. Leroy wondered why the Borough didn't just dig them all up.

Beyond the verge were the back gardens of the houses on the avenue, separated by a wire fence from the school grounds. They were big houses with big gardens. The houses themselves could barely be seen for the trees and bushes that crowded the gardens.

'You see that?' Calamity whispered excitedly.

He had stopped and was gazing bright-eyed across at one of the gardens.

Leroy stopped and looked as well. He couldn't see anything to get worked up about: just trees, a broken-down shed, a collapsing bit of trellis.

'What you on 'bout?' he demanded sourly.

'There!' Calamity hissed.

He butted his head several times in the direction of the garden. There were other pupils coming down the drive so he didn't want to make it too obvious.

Leroy narrowed his eyes and inspected the garden inch by inch. He still couldn't understand why Calamity was so excited.

'On the trees,' Calamity cried. He was getting annoyed.

Then Leroy saw them. Hanging in clumps of three or four. Weighing down the branches. Green ones and red ones and strange brown ones. Apples! There were five or six trees of them. Absolutely covered. How could he have missed them? His mouth began to water at the sight of them.

That was when Calamity came out with his idea. Though he didn't need to say anything. Leroy already knew what the idea was.

'Let's pinch some,' Calamity said.

Leroy gave his friend a hard stare. Not only was Calamity a walking disaster-area, he was thick as well. The drive was still busy with pupils, not to mention teachers. There was no break in the stream.

''Ow can we?' Leroy demanded scornfully. 'We ain't invisible, you know.'

'We could 'ang about till everyone's gone,' Calamity suggested.

Leroy looked at him pityingly. Calamity was getting worse. Leroy tried to be patient.

'Don' you t'ink it gonna look a bit suspicious?' he said gently. 'Us standin' 'ere on our own fo' hours just twiddlin' our thumbs?'

'Yeah,' Calamity agreed sadly. 'I suppose so.'

He cast a longing glance in the direction of the apple trees. His face and body had gone into a dejected droop.

He tried once more. 'You think it'll take long for everyone to go? You know 'ow they all rush off 'ome soon as the bell goes.'

'It'll take hours,' Leroy told him definitely. 'Besides, I gotta collect Paulette.'

That was it, then. Calamity reluctantly surrendered to the inevitable.

Leroy was disappointed too. Compared with some of Calamity's ideas, this one seemed quite reasonable. The apples certainly did look tempting, hiding among the leaves, twinkling as the wind swung the branches and the sun caught their glossy skins. They couldn't have been more than twenty yards away. So near, and yet so far.

As they walked down the drive, past the caretaker's house to the front gates, the apples were still in Leroy's thoughts. He could just imagine plucking them from the branches. The firm feel of them. The way they broke from the tree and came away in his hand. He could just imagine sinking his teeth into them, the juice spurting out and running down his chin. His mouth was watering again.

Calamity must have been thinking about them as well because, as they reached the gates, he had his second idea.

'Say,' he said, 'why don't we come up tonight an' pinch 'em? When it's dark.'

His eyes searched Leroy's face eagerly for approval.

Leroy thought about it. He knew all Calamity's ideas ended in disaster, but the taste of the apples was still in his mouth.

'I don' know if I can get away,' he said, trying to find a way out. 'My mum don' like me goin' out at night. She say it ain't safe.'

Calamity sensed that Leroy was weakening. 'Aw, come on,' he coaxed. 'Just think of it. All those apples. Just waitin' to be picked.'

'I don' know 'ow I'm gonna get out,' Leroy said again, still struggling.

'You'll find a way,' Calamity encouraged him.

Leroy gave in. 'OK. I tries to make it.'

'Great!' Calamity cried with delight. ''Ere at the gate. Eight o'clock. See you then.' And he was off before Leroy could have second thoughts.

As he walked down the avenue to Beechcroft Junior School, Leroy wondered gloomily what he had let himself in for.

All evening, he went on worrying about it. How was he going to get out?

At dinner, Mum had looked at him suspiciously and said, 'You very quiet. You all right?'

Dad was on the late shift.

'Yeah, Mum,' Leroy replied wearily.

''E's worried 'cause 'e can' do 'is 'omework,' jeered Floyd.

'No I ain't,' Leroy snapped.

How come Floyd knew he had French homework?

'Now you stop it, you two,' Mum commanded. 'I got enough to contend wit' wit'out that.'

'I wish I 'ad 'omework,' cried Paulette.

'Don' worry,' said Floyd. 'You will. Soon enough.' He hated having to do homework.

Later, Floyd went to work in his bedroom, and Leroy settled down to his French in the living room while Paulette watched television. Except he couldn't settle down to it. He kept being drawn to the screen to see what was happening. And he kept trying to work out how he could slip away without being noticed.

He realised the best time would be when Mum was putting Paulette to bed. It was ideal. Mum would be busy. She wouldn't notice if he was there or not. He could just slide out of the door.

Of course, there would still be the problem of getting back again. He wasn't sure how that was going to be managed. He might be able to get out without being detected, but Mum was sure to notice he wasn't there. And then when he came back there would be trouble.

That was the way with Calamity's ideas. They always produced problems. Still, he would worry about that later. After all, he had given Calamity his word. Well, sort of. He couldn't let him down.

'Come on, madam,' Mum said, switching off the television.

'Aw, Mum,' Paulette protested. 'It ain't finish yet.'

'Tough,' said Mum. 'It's time fo' you' bed.'

Paulette went on protesting, but she went.

This was the moment, Leroy thought. He closed his books and took them into his bedroom. Floyd was lying on his bed plugged into his Walkman.

'I t'ought you was suppose to be doin' you' 'omework,' Leroy said.

'What?' Floyd yelled, easing away an earphone.

'Oh, never mind,' Leroy muttered.

He opened the wardrobe and took out his parka. He was already wearing a sweater and jeans. Mum always made him change out of his school uniform as soon as he got home so as to keep it clean.

Floyd was watching him.

'Where you goin'?' he demanded.

'Mind you' own business,' Leroy retorted.

'Do Mum know?'

Leroy groaned. Floyd was a pain at times.

'I gonna meet Terry,' Leroy said. 'We got somet'in' to work out.'

But when he turned round, he saw that Floyd's eyes were shut and his head was nodding to the beat of his Walkman. From the bathroom came the sound of splashing water. The coast was clear. Leroy quickly let himself out of the front door and closed it quietly behind him.

As he padded down the stairs and across the estate, he found himself worrying. Up till then, he hadn't really thought of the dangers ahead. He was more concerned about whether Mum would notice he had gone and what would happen when he got back. Perhaps he should have asked Floyd to cover up for him. Perhaps his brother would anyway, though it wasn't likely.

But now, moving through the deserted shopping centre and up the avenue towards the school, all kinds of fears crowded in. How were they going to get into the garden? What chance was there of being caught? What would they do if they were?

It was typical of Calamity to jump into it with both feet without working out a plan.

By the time Leroy reached the school gates, he felt like telling Calamity to forget about it. Who wanted apples anyway? He was going off the idea. Rapidly. He would tell

Calamity so. But, of course, Calamity wasn't there.

Leroy began to fume. Now what was he to do? He had a good mind to turn right round and go back home. He walked up and down a few times trying to decide whether or not to stay.

He looked at his watch. It was almost a quarter past eight. He would give Calamity two more minutes. And if he hadn't turned up by then, it was all off and he would go home.

He watched sternly as the digits clicked past and eight-fifteen arrived. He lowered his arm and breathed out a furious snort. That was it then.

At that moment, he saw Calamity come racing up the avenue towards him.

'Sorry about that,' Calamity panted as he pounded to a halt beside Leroy. 'I couldn't get a bus. I 'ad to walk. I been runnin' all the way.'

Leroy shot him a sceptical glance, but all he said was, 'Come on then.' Since they were here they might as well go ahead – and get it over with.

It was then that they came across the first snag. Leroy had an ominous feeling it was going to be the first of many. The gates were locked.

Leroy had noticed they were closed when he arrived. But he had thought nothing more about it. They would be easy to push wide enough for them to slip through, he'd imagined. He hadn't noticed the padlock and chains.

'It's locked,' Calamity cried.

Leroy felt he exhibited great self-control.

'I knows that,' he said. 'So what we do now?'

'Climb over,' said Calamity, as though it were the simplest thing in the world.

Leroy ran his eyes up the gates. They must have been eight feet high at least. And they were under the full glare of the street lamp. He wished he hadn't come.

'We'll be seen,' he protested.

'Nobody's gonna see us,' Calamity said with astonishing confidence.

And before Leroy could argue any more, Calamity had thrown himself at the gates and was hauling himself up hand over hand.

Leroy looked quickly up and down the avenue. A car passed. The driver must have seen Calamity, but the car just went on.

Leroy gave up. He clung to the metal railing and pulled himself up. There was nothing else he could do. Calamity had already dropped down on the other side.

The gates juddered and rattled, but Leroy made it to the top. They hadn't shaken as much as that when Calamity had climbed up, but then Calamity was lighter. Leroy hung on as the gates swayed and arranged himself to jump. His feet hit the ground with a thud that sent shocks up his spine. He wondered if he would ever be able to walk again.

He straightened himself and found he could lift one foot in front of the other. Just.

Calamity was rapidly walking up the drive. He looked back.

'Come on,' he urged him in a loud whisper.

Leroy hobbled after him.

On their right was the caretaker's house. The downstairs windows were lit up, and they could hear the blare of the television.

'Shush,' warned Calamity, though Leroy hadn't said anything. 'Don't want old Carter to 'ear us.'

Everyone knew Mr Carter, the caretaker. He was always chasing boys out of the lavatories, confiscating footballs on the playground and accusing pupils of writing things on the walls. Leroy had no wish to meet him. He was broad and burly. If he hadn't been a caretaker, Leroy could imagine him humping barrow-loads of bricks on a building site.

They went further up the drive. Leroy noticed that Calamity was moving carefully, stride by stride on the tips of his toes. His head was going backwards and forwards with the effort. He must imagine he's in the SAS, Leroy thought.

The drive was in darkness. Mr Carter had forgotten to put

the lights on. Or else there was another economy drive on saving electricity.

They veered off the roadway and crossed the grass verge to the boundary fence. But it was difficult finding the right garden.

'It's 'ere somewhere,' said Calamity.

Leroy held back his exasperation. Of course it was here. It couldn't have got up and walked.

They edged their way along the fence, peering in at the trees and bushes.

'This is it, ain't it?' Calamity asked hopefully.

Leroy studied the garden doubtfully. He wasn't sure. It was all so dark and shadowy. Then a gust of wind swept across the trees. Some of the branches began to sway, and he could make out something shining out from them.

'Yeah, I think it must be,' he said.

'Right,' cried Calamity, his confidence restored. 'Let's get at 'em.'

He charged at the fence and clambered over.

Leroy couldn't help feeling they ought to be taking it all more cautiously. But it was too late to suggest that now. All he could do was climb over the fence after Calamity.

Under foot, the ground was thick with grass and weeds and uneven. But it wasn't too difficult to wade across it to the trees.

They didn't have to climb the trees either. The branches were so heavy with fruit that they hung down practically to the ground. All they had to do was reach out.

Calamity grabbed an apple and pulled it away. He bit into it and chewed.

'Tastes good,' he declared, still chomping away and wiping his mouth with the back of his hand.

'Shush,' warned Leroy. There were lights on in the house just visible through the trees. 'You don' want everyone to know.'

He plucked an apple and tested it. Calamity was right. It did taste good. Sweet and juicy.

Calamity had thrown away his apple half-eaten and was busy picking apples and stuffing them inside his track-suit top. Leroy began to do the same. Soon his parka was bulging. But Calamity was still hard at it, grabbing apples with both hands and shoving apples, leaves, twigs and all inside his track-suit top. He was beginning to look like that rubber man they used in tyre adverts. At this rate, the seams would burst or the zip would give way. It would take him a month to get through that lot.

'Come on,' said Leroy. 'We got enough.'

'OK,' said Calamity as he seized two more apples.

They scrambled back over the fence and strolled towards the front gates, munching away happily. They had to keep one hand clasped to their waists to make sure their booty didn't drop out.

'That was easy,' Calamity said smugly. He licked round his mouth to remove some bits of apple. 'I knew it was gonna be all right.'

'Yeah,' said Leroy.

He was feeling easier now it was over. Perhaps he had misjudged his friend. Perhaps not all his ideas turned out to be disasters after all. Perhaps he should tell him so.

But had he done so, he'd have spoken too soon.

They were just passing the caretaker's house when the door opened. Mr Carter stood lit up in the doorway.

That wasn't so bad. They were still hidden in the darkness of the drive. They could still have made a bolt for it.

But a little dog came charging out of the house and made straight for them. It must have had X-ray eyes. It circled round and round them, leaping up and yapping its head off. It wasn't much more than a foot in length, yet it seemed to think it was a tiger or something, and it was making enough noise to wake the whole avenue.

Leroy and Calamity tried to get away, but at every step they took, the dog danced around them, shot in at their ankles and darted back again, without ceasing its high-pitched barking. They didn't know where to put their feet for fear of treading on the beast.

Then Mr Carter was down on them. The dog went obediently and sat beside him and continued to growl.

Together, the two looked absurd. The tiny dog and the brawny man. Mr Carter probably had a dog as small as that to make him appear even bigger. Leroy would have laughed if he hadn't been so worried.

'What you doin' 'ere?' the caretaker demanded. 'What you up to?'

'Nothin',' said Calamity. 'We was just takin' a short cut.'

Leroy had to admire him for that. It was quick thinking all right. Not that it seemed to cut much ice with Mr Carter.

'Pull the other one,' he said. 'You're up to no good, I know it.'

'No, honest,' Calamity protested. 'We wanted to get to the avenue, and we didn't want to go all the way round so we climbed over the back gate and come past the school.'

'You know you ain't supposed to do that,' Mr Carter told them. 'It's breakin' an' enterin'. I could 'ave the police on to you for that.'

But he didn't sound too fierce. Leroy had a feeling they were in luck. They were going to get away with it.

'Don't do it again,' Mr Carter said.

'No, Mr Carter,' said Calamity, acting all relieved and grateful. 'We won't. Don't you worry.'

He raised his hand in a jaunty farewell.

And then it happened.

Leroy watched horror-struck as first one apple and then another slipped from the waistband of Calamity's track suit. Calamity clutched at his stomach with both hands, but it was too late. The apples were rolling down the drive, and the dog was chasing after them, sniffing and yapping. Mr Carter had a look of smug satisfaction on his face.

'So that's it, is it?' he said. 'I thought you looked an odd shape. I knew you was up to somethin'.'

He shot his hand out and tugged at the zip of Calamity's jacket. Apples came tumbling out onto the drive, and

bounced and rolled about. The dog jumped and raced after them.

'And you,' Mr Carter said as he turned to Leroy.

He pulled down the zip on Leroy's parka, and more apples poured out. The dog barked and leaped about, excited and delighted.

Calamity was hanging his head and looking ashamed. Leroy thought he'd better do the same.

'A fine thing,' Mr Carter was saying. 'Climbin' over the back gate is one thing. Takin' a short cut is one thing. But scrumpin' apples is somethin' else altogether. It's stealin'.'

The caretaker seemed to be enjoying himself.

'An' we can't 'ave that. I'll 'ave to report you to your form teacher. An' I bet 'e'll give you a good goin' over. An' quite right too. Now what's your names and which forms are you in. An' you needn't give me any false names neither 'cause I'll know you again all right. Don't you worry. I'll track you down, so you might as well give me your real names right away.'

Leroy and Calamity told him in a mumble.

'Brown an' Callum. I'll remember them all right. Don't you worry. You'd better 'op it now before I change my mind an' call the police.'

Leroy gave Calamity a scowl. Now he'd really landed them in it. Wait till he got him on his own.

He began to move towards the gates.

But Calamity was still waiting.

'Ain't you gonna open 'em?' he asked Mr Carter.

The caretaker didn't seem to know what he meant.

'The gates,' explained Calamity.

'Cheeky blighter!' exclaimed Mr Carter. 'I ain't unlockin' 'em. You climbed over 'em to get in, so you can climb over 'em to get out.'

'But we might damage 'em,' Calamity persisted.

'You damage 'em, an' you'll be in more trouble,' Mr Carter warned him.

He stood and watched as Leroy and Calamity walked

down the drive and began to grapple with the gates. The dog stood and watched too.

Leroy dejectedly pulled himself up. He swung his leg over the top and dropped to the road on the other side. Once again, the shock of his landing juddered up his spine.

He was feeling deflated. He couldn't even summon up enough energy to let Calamity have a bit of his mind. If Calamity hadn't been so cocky and made a big thing of waving goodbye, they might have got away with it. Trust Calamity to overdo it. But it wasn't worth bothering with that now.

And anyway, Calamity was looking so down in the mouth that Leroy didn't have the heart to have a go at him.

'Sorry about that,' Calamity mumbled.

'It weren't you' fault,' said Leroy.

And perhaps it wasn't. If it hadn't been for Mr Carter and that stupid dog . . .

They stood for a moment before going their separate ways. As he turned to go, Leroy noticed that Mr Carter was stooping down to pick up the apples that were strewn over the drive.

Talk about ill-gotten gains! That was a kind of stealing too, wasn't it?

Leroy walked home glumly, convinced there was no justice in the world.

Mum was waiting for him. Leroy knew she would be.

'Where you been?' she wanted to know.

Leroy had spent the whole journey home working out his answer.

'I 'ad to see Terry 'bout somet'in',' he told her innocently.

Well, it was more or less true.

'Why don' you tell me when you goes out?' Mum scolded. 'You gettin' bad as Floyd. You knows I don' like you goin' out when it dark. Not wit' all them t'iefs an' muggers 'bout.' She sniffed. 'Not to mention the police.'

'I were OK,' Leroy reassured her.

'More luck than good judgement I shouldn't wonder,'

Mum retorted. 'Now it's time you was in bed.'

Leroy congratulated himself on having got away with it. But not for long. He remembered what Mr Carter had said. There would be more trouble in the morning.

It must have been preying on Calamity's mind as well if the worried frown on his face next morning was anything to go by.

And the first thing he said was, 'D'you think old Carter's told Mr Baxter?'

'I don' know, do I?' Leroy retorted. Then he added, 'Probably.'

From his experience of life, the worst was bound to happen.

But Mr Baxter didn't say anything when he came into the classroom. He just began to call the register as usual.

'I reckon it'll be all right,' Calamity said, beginning to regain his confidence.

Leroy wished he wouldn't say things like that. It was tempting providence.

And sure enough, just as Calamity was cheering up and saying, 'I think we ought to try again', there was a knock at the door, and Mr Carter walked in.

Calamity stopped speaking, his mouth wide open. Leroy tried to shrink behind his desk.

Mr Baxter looked up at the burly figure of Mr Carter advancing towards him. Leroy was sure the teacher's eyes flickered with apprehension behind his gold-rimmed spectacles. But Mr Baxter stood up and greeted Mr Carter with a pleasant 'Good morning'. Mr Carter was twice as wide as Mr Baxter.

'I got a bone to pick with you,' Mr Carter said grimly, ignoring the greeting.

Leroy was sure Mr Baxter's face went a shade paler.

Mr Baxter swallowed. 'Oh, have you?' he stuttered. 'I'm sorry to hear that.'

'It's two o' your boys,' Mr Carter went on.

By now, the whole class was listening with awed attention.

'Oh dear,' cried Mr Baxter. 'Have they been misbehaving?'

'I'll give you misbe'avin',' Mr Carter boomed threateningly.

Mr Baxter jerked his head back as though afraid he was about to be assaulted.

But instead of doing that, Mr Carter drew one of his hands from behind his back and held it out. It was a great ham of a fist. Slowly, he uncurled the fingers and revealed an apple resting on the palm.

'What d'you think o' that?' he asked proudly as if he had just performed a miraculous conjuring trick.

Mr Baxter obviously didn't know what to think. 'It's an apple!' he said after some time.

Mr Carter breathed out with exasperation. 'Course it's an apple,' he exclaimed. 'But 'ow come it falls into my 'ands?'

Mr Baxter raised his eyes to the ceiling as though imagining a tree. But then he thought better of it. 'I really don't know,' he said.

'Well, it were two o' your lads,' Mr Carter informed him.

Mr Baxter still didn't quite get the picture. 'Two of my lads?'

'Yeah. I caught 'em last night. They climbed over the gate an' went scrumpin' in one o' the gardens backin' on to the drive.'

At last Mr Baxter understood. 'Oh, I see.'

He turned his gaze to the boys in the class and ran his eyes over them for signs of guilt. Leroy stared at the top of his desk and stayed very still.

'D'you know who they were?' Mr Baxter asked.

'Yeah. Brown an' Callum.'

Leroy lifted his head and put on a show of amazement.

'Yeah,' said Mr Carter with satisfaction. 'That's one o' 'em.'

Mr Baxter fixed Leroy with a frown of disapproval.

'An' I 'ope you give 'em what for,' said Mr Carter.

'Yes, I certainly will,' said Mr Baxter grimly.

'Right,' said Mr Carter. 'I'll be on me way.'

He threw the apple into the air and caught it.

He gave Mr Baxter a challenging glance. 'Now you've seen the evidence, I suppose there's no 'arm in takin' it away with me?'

'Oh, of course not, Mr Carter,' Mr Baxter was quick to respond.

With a smirk at Leroy and Calamity, the caretaker swaggered out of the classroom.

Not that Leroy had much time to observe Mr Carter's departure. He was holding himself ready for the storm that was bound to break.

'Leroy and Terence, come out here,' Mr Baxter rapped.

Leroy and Calamity awkwardly clambered to their feet and went to stand in front of the teacher's desk.

'Now, what have you got to say for yourselves?' Mr Baxter demanded.

Leroy hoped that Calamity would say something. But there was just silence. Calamity must have been waiting for Leroy to speak.

'Come on now,' said Mr Baxter impatiently. 'Is what Mr Carter said correct?'

'Yes, sir,' Leroy mumbled.

'Yes, sir,' Calamity agreed.

Mr Baxter let out a weary sigh. 'Well, I'm ashamed of you both. Letting me down like this. And the school. Don't you know we get complaints all the time from people who live round the school?'

Leroy didn't know.

'About balls going into their gardens. And pupils breaking their fences and trampling all over their flowers. And littering the place with their drink cans and crisp packets and sweet wrappers. About windows being broken. And now this.'

Leroy hung his head. He was thinking, I don't do any of these things. But there was no point in saying that now. Not with the mood Mr Baxter was in. He was getting really worked up.

'I think it's disgraceful. Giving the school a bad name like that. No wonder the people who live round the school never have anything good to say about us. No wonder they want to send their children to some other school. I'm ashamed of you.'

There was a lull. Leroy raised his eyes. Mr Baxter seemed to have run out of steam. His face was all puffed up and disapproving.

'Well, we'll have to do something,' he said at last. 'You'll have to apologize, that's what.'

'But they don' know we pinch their apples,' Leroy pointed out.

'Oh, don't they?' retorted Mr Baxter. 'Well, they soon will.'

Leroy wished he'd kept quiet.

'Yes,' said Mr Baxter with satisfaction. 'That's what you'll do. You'll apologize.'

'Yes, sir,' said Leroy.

'Yes, sir,' Calamity repeated.

They surrendered to the inevitable, breathed in deeply and made for the door.

'Where are you going?' Mr Baxter cried.

Leroy turned round and blinked with surprise. 'We was doin' what you said. We was goin' to apologize.'

'Not now,' groaned Mr Baxter. 'Not during school time. You can do it in your own time. Do it at lunch break.'

'Yes, sir,' mumbled Leroy.

'Yes, sir,' Calamity echoed.

They went and sat down. It seemed a long time to wait.

In the course of the morning, Veronica Wright made a point of loudly saying to her friend, Angie, 'I think it's dreadful stealin' apples.'

Leroy glowered at her, but she went on. 'Those poor people, lookin' after their trees all year, an' prunin' 'em, an' waterin' 'em, an' carin' for 'em, an' doin' whatever it is they

do to 'em, an' lookin' forward to the fruits o' their labour, an'
what do they find? All their apples 'as been pinched. It's not
right.'

'Yeah,' agreed Angie. 'I wouldn't accept no apology. I'd
call the police.'

'An' serve 'em right,' spat Veronica vindictively.

Leroy wished he hadn't heard. Supposing when they went
to apologize, the people did call the police. He couldn't enjoy
his lunch for thinking about it. He didn't speak to Calamity
much either. It was all his fault. Him and his ideas!

'Suppose we better go then,' Calamity said as he sucked
the last smear of custard off his spoon and put it down.

'Yeah,' said Leroy gloomily. 'Suppose so.'

They took their plates back to the hatch and set off down
the drive.

'What d'you think they gonna say?' Calamity asked nervously.

''Ow do I know?' Leroy snapped back.

'D'you think they'll call the police?'

So Calamity had heard Veronica as well and had been
worrying.

'Course not,' said Leroy. Though he didn't feel confident.

When they reached the avenue, they were faced with
another problem. They couldn't work out which was the
right house. The houses looked quite different from the front.

'It's this one,' said Calamity, pointing to a house with
pillars on either side of the front door.

'No it ain't,' Leroy cried, though he wasn't sure. 'We
ought to 'ave counted 'em from the back, an' then we would
'ave known.'

He walked along to the next house. The garden looked
neglected and overgrown. The windows were grimy and the
net curtains were grey with dirt. The paint on the door and
the window ledges was cracked and peeling.

'I t'ink it's this one,' he said, though he didn't know why.

'OK,' said Calamity, ready to give way to Leroy's super-
ior knowledge.

Leroy stared at the front gate for a moment. He wasn't looking forward to the ordeal ahead. But he was worried too about what would happen when he touched the dry withered wood of the gate. It looked as though it would come away in his hand or drop off its hinges.

He took the risk and pushed the gate open gently. It stayed in one piece.

They walked up the path. To judge from the weeds thrusting up between the flagstones and flourishing into flower, it seemed likely that not many people walked up that path.

Close to, the front door looked even more dilapidated.

There were cobwebs in the corners with dead leaves caught in them. The doorstep too was littered with leaves and dirt. What kind of person lived here, Leroy wondered. Not the kind of person who would welcome boys climbing into his garden and stealing his apples, he feared.

'You ring,' said Calamity.

Leroy gave him a cool stare. Wasn't that just like him?

He stretched out his hand and pressed the bell. He could hear it echoing loud and clear inside the house. It was almost as though the house were empty.

They waited, but no one came.

'Try again,' Calamity urged.

Leroy felt like kicking him. Why did it always have to be him who did it? Even so, he pressed the bell once more. They listened as the sound reverberated through the house.

Leroy had a sudden surge of hope.

Calamity must have had the same idea, because he whispered, 'Maybe there ain't nobody 'ere.'

'Yeah,' breathed Leroy.

It was funny how they were whispering.

Then there was a clatter that made them jump. Someone was undoing the bolts. The door creaked open a crack and a face appeared.

Leroy was shocked. The old woman's face looked as though it were made of lizard skin. It was like parched earth that had been cracked by the heat of the sun. Her hair was thin and grey and stuck up untidily all over her head. Her eyes were bleary and unfocused, the pupils wandering about. Leroy had never before been so close to anyone who looked so old.

The woman's eyes narrowed and her gaze came to rest on the faces in front of her. She opened her mouth as though to speak, but nothing came out. She tried again, and this time there was a croak.

'What do you want?' She sounded like an unoiled hinge that hadn't been used for years. It was eerie. Leroy didn't know whether to answer or to make a run for it. He wasn't sure if his voice was in a fit state to answer. But he managed it.

'We're from the school,' he said. 'From Beechcroft High.'

After what Mr Baxter had told them what local people thought of the school he suddenly wondered if that had been the best way to begin.

The old woman's eyes had started hovering unsteadily again. She let them wander down to the badges on their blazers. She seemed to recognize them.

'Oh yes,' she said, and it sounded almost human this time. 'I remember . . .'

She stopped in mid-sentence, unclear what it was she did remember.

Leroy cleared his throat. Having started, he would have to go on. But how? Calamity was being useless as usual. He was just standing there, staring at the old woman as though he was seeing a ghost.

'It's 'bout you' apples,' Leroy said at last.

The woman's face went blanker than it had been before, if that were possible.

'Apples?' She spoke the word as though she wasn't quite sure what it meant.

Leroy wondered if he had picked the wrong house after all. But he would have to get it over with now.

'Yeah,' he said, and then went on in a rush. 'We climb over you' fence last night an' pinch some o' you' apples, an'

Mr Carter – 'e's the caretaker – 'e catch us an' 'e tell Mr Baxter – 'e's our form teacher – an' 'e tell us we 'as to come an' apologize, an' that's what we're doin', we're apologizin'.'

By the end of it, Leroy was sweating.

'Apples?' the woman said.

She was still stuck at that word. She hadn't heard or understood a thing Leroy had been saying.

He took a quick look at Calamity. He had the feeling his friend had had enough and was getting ready to make a quick get-away. But Leroy decided he ought to stick it out. He was sure the old woman would get the message in the end.

'Yeah,' he said. 'You got apple trees in you' back garden.'

'Have I?' the woman asked. She sounded surprised.

Calamity was shuffling his feet and beginning to edge away.

'Yes, of course I have,' the woman cried as her memory came back to her. 'I'd forgotten. I haven't been out there for ages.'

Now they were getting somewhere, Leroy thought. He told his tale again.

'So you see, we're sorry,' he concluded.

From the look on her face, she seemed to have got it this time.

'Well,' she said, 'if you want some apples, you only have to ask. I never touch them myself. I don't like them much. And anyway, my teeth aren't what they were. So they just go rotten on the trees otherwise.'

At least she wasn't telling them off. Even Calamity seemed relieved.

'Would you like to get some now?' the woman asked.

Leroy suddenly brightened up. So did Calamity. This was a turn-up for the books all right.

'Yeah, OK,' said Calamity.

'Thanks,' said Leroy.

'Come in then.'

The woman drew the door wide to let them in. She led

them with slow steps along a passageway to a back room. Leroy couldn't help noticing the worn carpet and the dust collecting in corners. There was a musty smell too as though the windows hadn't been opened for years.

The back room was crowded with furniture. There was hardly space to move between it all. A divan against one wall had bedclothes strewn all over it. Leroy got the impression this was the only room in the house that the woman used, and she had had all her prized possessions brought there so she could have them round her.

A set of French windows looked on to the back garden. The woman groped her way across the room, clutching at tables and chairs for support. She began to grapple with the bolts that secured the doors at top and bottom.

'You'll have to help me with these,' she said as she fell back panting. 'I can't think when I last opened them.'

The bolts were certainly stiff, but after an effort Leroy managed to get them moving. He swung the doors outwards. Outside was a patio overgrown with weeds like the path to the front door, and then a wilderness of long grass and trees.

'You'll need something to put them in,' the woman said. 'Just a minute.'

She pulled open a drawer in a table and began to rummage inside. It was full of wrapping paper and bags carefully folded and pieces of string wound up in neat bundles.

'Waste not, want not,' the woman said, noticing Leroy's curious glance.

She drew out two plastic bags and handed them to Leroy and Calamity.

'These ought to be big enough.'

They were. They were the kind of bags you put shopping in.

'Off you go then. Take as many as you like.'

It was funny. She didn't look nearly so old and dopey now.

Leroy and Calamity didn't need to be told a second time. They waded through the grass to the apple trees, leaving wide wakes behind them. That was what the Red Sea would have looked like when Moses divided it, Leroy thought, remembering one of Mr Duffy's favourite stories.

They set to with a will. Apple after apple came away from the branches with a twist and a tug and went into the bags. Calamity was quite jubilant.

'Who'd have thought it would turn out like this,' he cried. 'It's one in the eye for old Carter.'

'Yeah,' Leroy agreed thoughtfully. 'It were nice o' the ole lady to let us 'elp ourselves.'

'Yeah. I thought she was a bit creepy to start with, but I reckon she's all right.'

Soon Leroy's bag was almost full. But Calamity went on in a frenzy, reaching up again and again as first one apple and then another attracted his eye.

'Ain't you finish yet?' Leroy asked. 'You' eyes is bigger than you' belly.'

'It ain't every day you get a chance like this,' Calamity retorted. 'Might as well make the most o' it.'

At last, even Calamity was satisfied. He had to carry the bag supported from underneath instead of by the handles to make sure it didn't burst. They went back to the house.

'You have done well,' the woman exclaimed, eyeing their bags.

Leroy felt a sudden sweep of shame. Calamity really was a greedy pig! But there didn't seem to be anything behind the woman's words.

She went on. 'I remember what it was now. Beechcroft High. Those Christmas parties they had. For the old people round about. I did enjoy them. A lovely spread they laid on. And there was singing and dancing. And the pupils used to do turns and entertain us. And they sent a car to collect us and take us home again.'

It was good to know someone had something good to say about the school, Leroy thought. Especially after what Mr Baxter had said earlier on.

The woman was looking puzzled. 'I wonder what happened to them. The parties, I mean. It must be three or four years since I last went to one. I know there was one year I missed because I was ill, and then they didn't seem to bother with me any more.'

She gave an odd cackle. 'Perhaps they think I died.'

But she didn't sound depressed or upset or anything. Just

amused.

In fact, while they'd been there she'd changed. She was quite bright-eyed now and cheerful. Leroy was amazed. She looked twenty years younger than when she had first opened the door to them.

'I'll ask 'bout it,' Leroy said.

'Will you? That is kind of you. I should so like to go to one of those Christmas parties again. It would be something to look forward to. Tell them it's Mrs Leyton at No 56.'

'I'll do that,' said Leroy.

'We better be gettin' back,' Calamity warned him. 'We gonna be late.'

'We mustn't have that,' Mrs Leyton cried.

Leroy helped her to bolt the French windows again, and they made their way through to the front door.

'When you've finished those,' Mrs Leyton said, 'you can have some more. You only have to ask.'

Leroy and Calamity mumbled their thanks and hurried down the path.

As he shut the gate behind them, Leroy noticed that the old woman was still standing in the doorway. He waved goodbye, but she didn't respond. She didn't even seem to notice. It was as though she'd already forgotten who he was.

They heard the hooter announcing the beginning of afternoon school when they were only halfway up the drive. ''Urry up,' Leroy cried, and he began to run.

'Wait for me,' Calamity moaned.

Leroy looked over his shoulder to see Calamity struggling to catch up, lumbering along with his bag of apples in his arms like a wild baby.

Serve him right for being so greedy, Leroy thought, but he hung on until Calamity reached him.

'Say, what we gonna do with all these apples anyway?' Calamity panted. 'I can't eat 'em all.'

'Why didn' you t'ink 'bout that before?' Leroy retorted.

But there was no problem. As soon as the other pupils in 1B saw what Leroy and Calamity were carrying, there was a stampede, and they were surrounded by a deafening mob.

'Go on, give us one!'

'Ooh, let's 'ave an apple!'

'You lucky things! Ain't you gonna share 'em?'

''Ow you get them then?'

'Ooh, they taste good!'

Even Veronica Wright was persuaded to take one.

'Go on,' urged Angie. 'They're ever so nice.'

'Oh, all right,' Veronica said with a show of reluctance, and she spent a long time inspecting the apples in Calamity's bag before she picked the biggest one she could find.

Ms Graham was not pleased when the whole of 1B entered her classroom munching apples.

'In the bin!' she commanded, and there was thud after thud as apple cores were discarded.

She blamed Leroy and Calamity, of course.

'You better put those bags at the front by my desk,' she told them. 'And then no one will feel tempted to eat during the lesson.'

She supervised them closely while they did what she said.

But during the next lesson, Mr Weston was less observant. He didn't notice that Leroy and Calamity were carrying extra burdens. Nor did he notice apples being handed from hand to hand and chomped surreptitiously behind raised desk-lids.

By the end of the period, the bags were less than half full.

At registration, Mr Baxter asked Leroy and Calamity if they had apologized.

'Yes, sir,' Leroy told him.

'What happened?'

Leroy wondered how best to tell him. He had a feeling it hadn't gone quite the way Mr Baxter intended.

'She said it were all right,' Leroy said at last. 'She let us pick some apples.'

'She what?' Mr Baxter exploded.

Then he controlled himself. 'I see. Well, that was very decent of her.' Then he added with a severe look, 'And I hope that will be a lesson to you both.'

Leroy couldn't quite see what he meant.

'Do they still 'ave Christmas parties?' he asked.

Mr Baxter was obviously confused by the sudden change in subject. 'What are you asking about that for? It's far too early to be thinking of Christmas parties. There's nearly three months to go yet. We can decide whether we're having a form party nearer the time.'

'No,' said Leroy, 'it weren't that. I mean parties for old people.'

'Oh, I see. Yes, the sixth form arranges one every year. We're quite famous for them.'

'Mrs Leyton wants to come,' Leroy went on. And he explained how she had somehow got left off the list.

'I'll make a note of that,' said Mr Baxter. 'I'll make sure Mr Garfield knows. She won't be forgotten this time.'

Leroy noticed that Mr Baxter was watching him with a look of surprise on his face.

'That's very thoughtful of you, Leroy,' the teacher said.

'Oh, that's all right, sir,' Leroy told him.

As they walked down the drive, Calamity examined the contents of his bag.

'Ain't many left,' he said. 'An' most o' them's goin' mouldy.'

'Same 'ere,' said Leroy.

Then Calamity's face lit up. 'Say, I got an idea!'

Leroy heard the alarm bells clanging in his head again. Not another idea!

'What is it?' he asked cautiously.

'Why don' we give what's left over to old Carter?'

Leroy thought about the idea. He could just imagine the look on Mr Carter's face when they presented him with the left-over fruit. What was the expression Mr Duffy used? About heaping coals of fire. Perhaps there was some kind of justice in the world after all.

And in any case, they could always go back and get some more. Mrs Leyton had said so.

Perhaps he'd misjudged Calamity. Perhaps his ideas weren't all bad.

'Yeah,' he said. 'Let's.'

And a slow grin spread across his face.

Leroy's Song

'You know,' Mr Baxter said to Leroy one morning at the end of registration, 'there's a song about you.'

Leroy didn't know. He was brought up short. How could there be? Who'd dare write a song about him? And without so much as a by-your-leave too.

'Is there?' he asked cautiously.

'Yes,' said Mr Baxter. 'I heard it on the radio the other day.'

Leroy wasn't sure, but he had a feeling that Mr Baxter's mouth was trying hard not to break into a smirk, and his eyes behind his gold-rimmed spectacles were trying hard to remain steady.

'Oh, yeah,' Leroy said without committing himself. He didn't want to sound too ignorant, or too interested either, before he knew more.

'Yes,' said Mr Baxter. 'It's quite well known apparently. It's about bad Leroy Brown.'

Calamity exploded with laughter.

'That figures,' he spluttered.

Leroy fixed him with a glare.

'You ought to listen to it some time,' Mr Baxter said.

'Yeah,' said Leroy coolly. 'Maybe I'll do that.'

And he sauntered off to his first lesson.

But as soon as he was outside the door of his form room, he turned on Calamity. 'What's all this 'bout a song?' he demanded, as if it were all Calamity's fault.

'Search me,' cried Calamity. 'I dunno, do I? Maybe Mr Baxter's 'avin' a joke. Maybe 'e made it all up.'

But Leroy was not convinced.

'Naw, 'e don' do t'ings like that. 'E ain't got no sense o' 'umour.'

He brooded over it for a while and then burst out again indignantly, 'An' 'ow come 'e says it's 'bout me? What people writin' songs 'bout me fo'? That's what I wants to know.'

'Don't ask me,' said Calamity.

Then he gave Leroy a sly look. 'But whoever it is, 'e seems to know you all right. 'E got your number an' no mistake. *Bad* Leroy Brown.'

'Shut it,' Leroy snapped.

But Calamity just went on laughing.

For the rest of the day Leroy could think of nothing else. What really got him was the cheek of it. Somebody writing a song about him. Without his permission. Besmirching his character and broadcasting it all over the radio for everyone to hear. It wasn't right. There had to be a law against it, didn't there? He could have this person up for libel or slander or something. He could take him to court for damages. If he could only find out who it was.

But that was the problem. How did he find out? He couldn't listen to the radio all day waiting for the song to turn up again. He couldn't ask Mr Baxter more about it. There had been something about the way his form teacher's lips had twitched and his eyes had almost twinkled when he had first told him that made Leroy decide not to risk that.

So what could he do?

Then he remembered the record shop in the shopping centre. Perhaps they would have heard of it.

At the end of school, he collected Paulette and hurried her down the avenue to the shopping centre.

'What we rushin' fo'?' Paulette asked.

'I got business to do,' Leroy told her.

'What business?'

'Private.'

Paulette shrugged her shoulders and didn't ask any more.

When they got to the record shop, Leroy told her to wait and not go away.

'You buyin' a record?' Paulette asked, surprised.

'Maybe,' said Leroy.

'What!' Paulette cried as though he was mad.

'Well,' said Leroy defensively, 'ain't no 'arm in lookin'.'

He left Paulette puzzled and not quite believing him and went into the shop.

There was a boy behind the counter – Junior, a friend of Floyd's. Leroy was a bit put out by that. He hadn't been expecting it to be anyone he knew. Now it would be embarrassing.

He played for time by flicking through some of the record covers on the racks and skimming through the titles. But it was hopeless. There were hundreds of records. It was like looking for a needle in a haystack. There was nothing for it but to ask. Leroy gritted his teeth and went up to the counter.

'You got a record 'bout Leroy Brown?'

Junior looked blank. 'Leroy Brown?'

'Yeah,' said Leroy. He gritted his teeth harder. '*Bad* Leroy Brown.'

Junior shook his head. 'Never 'eard o' it.'

Ah well, Leroy thought. That was that. At least he'd tried. He turned to go.

And then Junior shouted after him. 'Hey, *you*'re Leroy Brown, ain't you?'

Leroy had to admit he was.

Junior began to get quite shirty at that. ' 'Ere, what you doin' wastin' my time an' 'avin' me on like that?'

'But I weren't,' Leroy protested. 'There's a song called *Leroy Brown*.'

'Oh no there ain't,' said Junior. 'D'you t'ink I'm stupid or somet'in'? Just you wait till I tells you' brother.'

'You tell 'im,' Leroy retorted, though he didn't fancy the idea much.

He banged out of the shop.

Paulette was waiting for him expectantly, but her face dropped when she saw he was empty-handed.

'You didn' buy no record then?' she asked.

'Naw,' said Leroy scornfully. 'Ain't none worth buyin'.'

As they walked home Leroy went on puzzling over this song. It was a mystery. Junior had said there was no such song, and he ought to know something about it working in a record shop. So what had Mr Baxter been on about? Had his form teacher been joking after all? Leroy just couldn't be sure. He went on worrying about it all evening.

Just as he was about to go to bed, Floyd got home. Mum had a go at him as usual.

'Where you been till this hour?' she demanded.

'I been out,' Floyd replied, all reasonable, as if that was an answer.

Mum blew out a great draught of air, wondered whether or not to explode, and then decided it wasn't worth the effort.

Floyd didn't even notice. He was grinning and prodding Leroy.

'Hey,' he said, 'what's all this 'bout some song?'

He must have seen Junior. Leroy wished he could vanish through the floor.

'Ain't not'in',' he muttered.

'Sound somet'in' to me,' Floyd cried. 'Ain't every day somebody write a song 'bout you.' And he creased up with laughter.

'Floyd!' Mum warned. 'You'll wake Paulette.'

'I were only 'avin' some fun,' Floyd protested, though not too loudly.

He shook his head sadly at Leroy. 'I don' know where you gets these ideas from. I can' t'ink why anybody'd want to write a song 'bout you. Now, Diane, maybe, or Michelle. I sure could make up some songs 'bout them myself. But you!'

He let out a wild hoot.

'Floyd!' Mum warned again.

Floyd covered his mouth with his hand but went on sniggering.

'Anyway,' he said when he had recovered, 'even if there is a song 'bout Leroy Brown, it don' mean it's 'bout you. There must be 'undreds o' Leroy Browns. Thousands probably.'

It wasn't something that had occurred to Leroy before. Well, it wouldn't, would it? The idea that there are lots of people walking around with the same name as you. No doubt Floyd was right. There probably were other people called Leroy Brown. But it didn't make it any better. It made it worse.

Leroy got to his feet with as much dignity as he could manage and said, 'I'm goin' to bed.'

It was one way of getting away from Floyd. At least he'd be asleep before Mum forced Floyd to stop watching television and go to bed as well. But he had the feeling his dreams were going to be filled with ghostly figures of Leroy Browns parading up and down before him. And not one of them would look anything like him.

Floyd kept up the joking for a few days, and then forgot about it.

After a while, Leroy forgot about it too. If there really was a song about Leroy Brown – this other Leroy Brown whoever he was – there didn't seem to be any way for him to find out about it.

And then, one afternoon a few weeks later, the song suddenly came back into his life.

It was lunch break, and he and Calamity were walking across the playground when Mr Garfield appeared. He seemed to have them in his sights. He was making straight towards them.

'Watch it,' Calamity warned.

But it was all right. Mr Garfield was in his post-lunch mood.

'Ah, there you are,' he cried, as though they were long lost friends. 'How are you getting on?'

'All right, sir,' Leroy mumbled. What else could he say?

'Now let me see,' said Mr Garfield, concentrating on Leroy. 'You've got a brother, haven't you?'

'Yes, sir.'

'Now don't tell me. Let me see if I can remember your name.'

Leroy stood patiently while Mr Garfield's face went into all sorts of contortions in an effort to force his brain to come out with the right name. Then his eyes popped wide and he gasped.

'Brown,' he cried. 'That's it, isn't it?'

'Yes, sir.'

'Now what's your first name again?'

Leroy opened his mouth to tell him.

'No!' Mr Garfield insisted. 'Don't say it. Let me guess.'

He closed his eyes and twisted his face into a knot as he searched his memory. Then his face cleared.

'I know,' he cried. 'It's Floyd.'

'No, sir,' said Leroy. ''E's my brother.'

'Of course he is,' said Mr Garfield, a touch sharply. 'I know that. So you must be . . . You must be . . . It's on the tip of my tongue. Yes, you must be . . .' Then he got it.

'You must be Leroy Brown. Just like the song.'

Leroy felt his heart miss a beat. There it was again. That song. He caught Calamity giving him an odd look.

'The song?' Leroy heard himself asking cautiously.

'Yes,' said Mr Garfield. '*Bad Bad Leroy Brown.*'

Leroy groaned inside. It was getting worse.

'Frank Sinatra made a record of it. Very good it is too.'

Leroy had heard of Frank Sinatra.

'Anyway,' said Mr Garfield, looking round the play-ground. 'Glad to hear you're getting on all right. Any problems, you come straight to me.'

'Yes, sir.'

Mr Garfield already had his eye on someone else he wanted to speak to and was on his way, weaving unsteadily towards him.

'So there *is* a song,' Calamity gasped. 'Mr Baxter weren't jokin'.'

'I told you 'e weren't,' said Leroy grandly, though worries about what the song might say came rushing back to him.

'And it's *bad* bad Leroy Brown now,' said Calamity with a leer.

'Oh yeah?' said Leroy scornfully. 'Well, that's somet'in' you would know 'bout, innit?'

And he strolled away as if that settled the matter, his head up high.

When school was over, he hurried to pick up Paulette and get down to the shopping centre. He had a clue now. Frank Sinatra. The record shop was bound to have Frank Sinatra records, and there was just a chance this song might be on one of them.

When he stopped outside the record shop, Paulette examined him reproachfully.

'You ain't gonna buy another record, is you?' she asked wearily.

'I'm just gonna 'ave a look,' he told her. 'Now you stay 'ere. I won' be long.'

As luck would have it, Junior was behind the counter again. Leroy gave him a nod without looking at him and made straight for the racks of records. They were arranged in alphabetical order under the names of singers and groups. And yes, there was Frank Sinatra's name. There were quite a few records, too. Ten in all. This Frank Sinatra must be popular.

Leroy took each cover out, turned it over and ran his eyes down the contents. By the time he had reached the eighth record, he was beginning to give up hope, and Junior was beginning to get impatient.

And then he saw it. There it was. *Bad Bad Leroy Brown*. It gave him quite a start to see his name in print like that. He stared at the song title in amazement. He'd only half believed it really existed.

He took the cover over to Junior at the counter.

'Play band seven fo' me,' he said. 'On the second side.'

Junior glanced at the cover and then stared at Leroy.

'You wants to 'ear this?' he exclaimed, his eyebrows rising with surprise.

'Yeah,' said Leroy stubbornly. 'I ain't buyin' somet'in' I ain't 'eard.'

Reluctantly Junior checked the number on the sleeve and searched along the shelves behind him for the record. He took it out of its protective cover and placed it on the turntable. He counted down to band seven without bothering to look at the titles and set it to play. Leroy settled himself on a stool and fitted the earphones.

First of all the drums and brass set up a beat and then the singer came in. Leroy's first reaction was that the song sounded as though it ought to have been sung by a black man. Still, this Frank Sinatra was doing the best he could. Then he concentrated on the words.

It was about bad bad Leroy Brown all right. He lived on the south side of Chicago which was apparently the worst part of town. And if you went down there, you had to take care in case you bumped into Leroy Brown. Because he was trouble – he was more than trouble. He was big, about six-feet-four tall, and all the ladies there fancied him, and all the men were polite to him and called him *sir*. He was a gambler and he liked to dress up in smart clothes. He liked diamond rings too and waved them in front of everybody, and he had two flash cars. In his pocket he kept a gun, and he had a razor in his shoe. He was real bad and mean.

Then one Friday about a week ago, the song went on, when Leroy was shooting dice, he saw a lady called Doris sitting at the edge of the bar, and he really liked the way she looked. And that was when the trouble started because the lady had a jealous husband. Leroy learned not to mess about with a lady like that.

The song didn't say, though, how he learned. Or what happened to him. It just went on saying how bad and mean he was.

Leroy listened, appalled. This wasn't him. This wasn't the Leroy Brown he knew. Well, he hadn't really expected it to be about him, but still it was a bit of a liberty to use his name for a character like this. A gambler, a gangster, a hoodlum. He was a real wicked man. It was defamation of character, wasn't it? It was taking his name in vain.

'You buyin' it?' Junior asked.

But Leroy was still suffering from shock. All he could do was give Junior a glazed stare.

Then he said, 'Play it again.'

He knew Paulette would be growing impatient waiting outside, but he had to hear those words once more.

Junior narrowed his eyes at Leroy and sucked his teeth slowly. But he set the turntable going.

This time as he listened, Leroy felt himself begin to warm to the song and the character. Maybe he wasn't so bad. In fact, he was quite something. He had a bit of style. Leroy imagined himself six-feet-four tall, flashing diamond rings about, driving swish cars, having all the ladies fall over him, and the men call him *sir*. That would have been all right. That would have been some life.

A pity about him getting into trouble, but still . . .

By the end of the song, Leroy's head was bobbing up and down, and he was smiling. Fancy Mr Garfield knowing a song like that. It was great. The song-writer was forgiven for using his name. In fact, Leroy felt quite proud that he had.

He took the earphones off and laid them on the counter. He slipped off the stool and started to walk out of the shop.

'Ain't you buyin' it?' Junior called sharply.

'I t'inks 'bout it,' Leroy replied.

And he got out quick.

Paulette was still there.

'You was a long time,' she said reproachfully.

'Yeah,' said Leroy. 'Sorry 'bout that. But there were this record I 'ad to 'ear.'

The words and music were still swirling round in his head. He drew himself up to his full six-feet-four. He fingered the diamond rings on his hands. He patted his pocket to make sure his gun was still there for when he needed it. He went off swinging down the street. All the ladies gave him admiring glances. All the men looked scared and got out of his way.

Paulette was tagging along beside him. She tugged at his hand.

'What record?' she asked.

Leroy came out of his dream.

'Oh, just some record 'bout Leroy Brown,' he told her casually.

'But that's you!' Paulette exclaimed.

'Yeah,' he said, and he smiled. 'Sort of. Maybe I buys it one day . . . when I gets a record player.'

A Day in the Country

'How many of you have ever seen a cow?' Mr Baxter asked 1B one day in that enthusiastic tone of voice he sometimes adopted.

You must be joking, Leroy thought. Where would you find cows round here?

And then he stared as Calamity's hand slowly crept upwards.

'Yes, Terence?' said Mr Baxter, his face hopeful.

'I seen a cow once,' Calamity told him.

Leroy scowled at him. He couldn't believe it.

'It was on television,' Calamity went on. 'Some programme about – '

But he couldn't finish. Whatever he was going to say was lost in a roar of derision from the class. Leroy joined in more loudly than anyone.

'No, no,' cried Mr Baxter, becoming flustered. 'Not that. I mean a real cow.'

'Well, this was a real cow,' Calamity persisted stubbornly. 'It wasn't dead or anythin'.'

'But you didn't see it in the flesh, did you?' asked Mr Baxter.

''Ow d'you mean?' Calamity demanded suspiciously.

Mr Baxter let out a tired sigh. 'It wasn't in the room with you, was it? You couldn't touch it or smell it or hear it mooing, could you?'

'I wouldn't want it in the room with me,' Calamity said sullenly. 'But it made a noise.'

'I've touched and smelled a camel,' Veronica Wright burst out. 'Ooh, it didn't 'alf pong. An' I've ridden on one. It was when we was in Tunisia on 'oliday. I couldn't sit down for a week after it, I was so sore.'

Trust Veronica Wright to start showing off again, Leroy thought.

'We're not talking about camels, Veronica,' said Mr Baxter, putting her down for once. 'We're talking about cows.'

'I just thought you'd like to know,' said Veronica huffily.

With any luck she'd sulk for the rest of the period.

Mr Baxter took a deep breath and started again.

'Now, forget about television. How many of you have been in the countryside and seen cows in fields?'

He waited expectantly. There were a few puckered faces as people tried to remember, but no hands went up.

'Ah ha!' he cried triumphantly. 'I thought as much. You go gallivanting off to places like Tunisia, and you haven't even explored the rural delights of England.'

Rural delights? What was he on about, Leroy wondered. And he'd never gallivanted off to Tunisia. But at least it was one in the eye for Veronica Wright.

'You're so parochial,' Mr Baxter went on, getting quite worked up.

(What was that, Leroy asked himself. It sounded rude.)

'You live in your own little worlds, bounded by streets in which you were born and brought up, breathing all those toxic fumes and car exhausts and lead-polluted air. And you don't even know there are corn fields and dairy herds and pig farms less than ten miles away. Where d'you think your milk comes from every morning?'

Leroy glanced across at Calamity. He had his mouth open. Leroy was sure he was about to say 'the Co-op', but luckily Mr Baxter hurried on.

'So that's why next Wednesday we're going on a visit to a farm.'

At last he had come to the point.

'We're going to see how your food is produced and smell some of that fresh country air.'

He awaited their response, like a conjuror who had just

drawn a rabbit out of a top hat.

Nobody said anything.

But Leroy was thinking. He didn't want to go and visit the countryside. What was there there? Just grass and trees and open space. And cows. It didn't interest him at all.

Meanwhile, Mr Baxter was going on trying to stir up enthusiasm, and giving them instructions. They had to bring sandwiches and something to drink. They would be away for the whole day. As a special treat, they wouldn't have to wear school uniform.

Well, Leroy thought, if it was Wednesday, they would miss maths and French. That was something.

'It's part of your course,' Mr Baxter said, trying to arouse some interest.

As if that helped. What use was the countryside anyway? With all that open space, it was bound to be draughty. And all you could do was look at it.

But it appeared that Mr Baxter had other ideas.

'We have a worksheet prepared for you,' he informed them.

Who was 'we', Leroy wondered.

'A kind of questionnaire. You'll have to find out things and make notes, and we're going to use the information you collect in the next few lessons.'

Leroy knew there would be a catch in it. So did some of the others. There were moans and protests.

Mr Baxter was quick to reassure them.

'But it won't be all work. You'll have a chance to relax and have a picnic.'

A picnic! In October! It would probably be raining.

And another thing, Leroy grumbled to himself. He'd miss his free dinner.

When he mentioned it to Mum, she had the same thought.

'They don' worry 'bout t'ings like that,' she complained 'when they 'as these fancy notions. 'Avin' to spend money on food fo' you so's you can romp round the countryside.'

Romp? Leroy wasn't going to romp.

'I don' see why you can' stay in you' classroom,' Mum went on, 'an' get a proper education.'

'It weren't my idea,' Leroy reminded her. He didn't see why he should take the blame.

'An' why didn' you tell me before?' Mum demanded, moving on to another cause for complaint.

Leroy had forgotten to tell her about the outing and the need for sandwiches until the evening before.

'It kinda slip my mind,' Leroy said by way of excuse.

'It sure is a good job you' 'ead is glued on 'ard,' said Mum, 'else you'd be forgettin' that.'

Leroy was about to sigh crossly, but a quick look at Mum's face made him change his mind.

'Now what kind o' t'ing does you want?' Mum asked.

'I don' know,' protested Leroy. 'It suppose to be a picnic.'

'A picnic? At this time o' year?'

'That's what I thought.'

'Well, what does the others 'ave when they 'as sandwich dinners at school?'

'All sort o' t'ings,' Leroy told her. Then he remembered Lalji. 'Chapattis stuffed wit' coleslaw an' cheese.' His mouth began to water at the thought of it. Lalji always brought those. He even let Leroy have a bit sometimes.

'Well, we're clean out o' chapattis,' Mum informed him drily. 'What else you fancy on the menu?'

'I don' know,' said Leroy, growing exasperated. 'Just sandwiches, I guess.'

Mum thought for a while. 'I could open a tin o' 'am, I suppose. That's if I 'as a tin o' 'am.'

Ham came from pigs, didn't it? Leroy wasn't sure what the pigs would feel when they saw him eating one of their relations.

But there had been too much moaning already for him to make any complaint.

Mum found she did have a tin of ham. She put it in the fridge to be ready for the morning.

There were more grumbles when Leroy appeared in the

kitchen for breakfast wearing a sweater and jeans.

Mum's eyes went round and she froze with horror. 'What do you t'ink you got on?' she demanded.

'We don' 'ave to wear school uniform,' Leroy explained.

Mum's eyes narrowed and bore through him searching for the truth.

'You sure?'

'Yeah, Mum.'

'It's all right fo' some,' Floyd muttered. 'Where you goin', anyways?'

Mum rounded on him.

'If you come 'ome nights, you'd know what goin' on in this 'ouse.'

Floyd collapsed in his chair with an inane grimace of pain on his face. But Mum had already turned her back.

When Floyd had recovered, Leroy told him about the outing.

'Oh, that,' Floyd said disdainfully. 'Mr Baxter take 'is class every year. I t'ink 'e just like a excuse fo' a day off.'

Then he remembered. 'I suppose to 'ave a lesson wit' 'im today. I 'opes Mr Garfield ain't takin' it.'

Paulette piped up. 'What you gonna bring me?'

Leroy looked at her cautiously. 'What d'you mean?'

'What you gonna bring me from the countryside? Ain't you gonna bring me a present?'

'I don' t'ink they grows presents in the countryside,' Leroy told her gruffly.

'An' that remind me,' said Mum. 'What 'bout Paulette? What time you suppose to be back, Leroy?'

'I don' know.'

'Floyd!' Mum roared threateningly.

But Floyd was ready for her. 'Aw, Mum,' he pleaded, his face creased with agony. 'I can' collect Paulette. I got t'ings to do after school.'

Mum let out an exasperated sigh. 'Ain't that always the way? I reckons I'll 'ave to do it myself.'

She jabbed a finger in Leroy's direction. 'An' that somet'in' else those teachers don' t'ink 'bout when they 'as these fancy ideas.'

They had been told to meet at the front gate of the school and wait for the coach there. The assembled mob in their jeans and sweaters and boots and anoraks and assorted hats looked ready for a polar expedition outfitted by Oxfam. Pupils in uniform trudging up to school gazed at them enviously.

'What you got?' Calamity asked Leroy.

''Am sandwiches, a Kit-Kat, a apple an' a can o' orange. 'Ow 'bout you?'

'I dunno,' said Calamity.

He reached inside his bag and pulled out a bulky parcel. Leroy watched with interest as his friend unwrapped it.

'Pork pie, cheese sandwiches, a Mars bar, two bananas an' a Coke,' Calamity told him.

Leroy licked his bottom lip.

'Swap you a 'am sandwich fo' a cheese one,' he suggested casually.

'OK.'

The exchange was made. And then there didn't seem to be much point in putting the sandwiches away again. It was at least an hour since either of them had had breakfast. Leroy took a big bite out of his sandwich and began to chew. Calamity did the same.

'That's supposed to be your picnic,' a voice reproved.

Leroy started guiltily.

Mr Baxter had arrived. He was staring at them disapprovingly.

'I were 'ungry,' Leroy said in defence.

'You'll be hungrier still by lunchtime,' Mr Baxter warned.

Reluctantly, Leroy and Calamity put their packed lunches away. Mr Baxter was always spoiling their fun.

But then Leroy's attention was caught by Mr Baxter's appearance. His eyes widened as he took in the teacher's gumboots, thick stockings, heavy jeans and the bulky polo-necked sweater that reached practically to his knees and flared out like a skirt.

Leroy was just about to nudge Calamity and point out this strange sight when Calamity nudged him. Ms Graham had arrived. She was wearing boots too – moon boots – and a padded jump suit, the kind skiers wear. On top of her head was a bobble hat, round her neck a woolly muffler, and on her hands a pair of thick mittens.

Leroy began to get worried. He looked at his own sweater and jeans. What was it like in the countryside? Did he have enough clothes on?

'Miss Graham's old Baxter's girlfriend,' Calamity confided.

'No, she ain't,' Leroy retorted scornfully, without having any idea whether she was or not.

'Course she is,' protested Calamity. ''E's round 'er all the time. Ain't you seen 'im on the playground talkin' to 'er when they're on duty? An' 'avin' lunch together? An' gettin' a lift off 'er in 'er car sometimes?'

'That don' mean not'in,' said Leroy. But he resolved to keep an eye open in future for any tell-tale signs.

The coach arrived, and there was a mad scramble to get on board. The driver scowled at them as they pushed past him. He looked as if he was in a bad temper.

'Now don't you leave no sweet papers or fag ends on the floor like you done last time,' he warned them.

Fag ends, Leroy thought. As if he would. He didn't smoke. He didn't approve of it. He'd tried it once.

Leroy and Calamity made a grab for the front seat, but Mr Baxter turfed them out.

'I'm sitting there,' he snapped.

'What, with Miss Graham?' Calamity asked with a leer.

'Yes, of course,' said Mr Baxter. 'With *Ms* Graham.' He didn't seem at all put out.

'What did I tell you?' gloated Calamity triumphantly as he and Leroy found a seat further up the coach. It didn't seem to Leroy like definite proof, though.

When they were all in, Mr Baxter stood up at the front and

yelled at them to be quiet.

'Now settle down, all of you. It'll take us about an hour, so just sit back and enjoy it. And I don't want any trouble. We have a very good reputation with this coach company, and I don't want it spoiled.'

Leroy could see the driver turning round and giving Mr Baxter an odd look.

An hour to reach wherever it was they were going! The countryside must be miles away, Leroy thought.

It took them at least half an hour to get clear of houses and shops. Bored, Leroy and Calamity swapped another sandwich.

Then the houses gave way to trees and hedgerows and fields.

'This is it,' Calamity cried. 'This is the countryside.'

'No, it ain't,' Leroy said scornfully. 'We got another 'alf hour to go.'

He bit into another sandwich.

Mr Baxter had calculated it about right. An hour after leaving the school, the coach turned into the yard of the farm they were to visit.

As soon as he stepped off the coach, Leroy could smell it. This was the countryside all right. The smell wasn't anything like it was at home. In fact, he wasn't sure if there was a smell round where he lived. Maybe he'd just got used to it.

But this place had a smell all right. It hit you right between the nostrils. It was animals and manure and rotting hay.

Leroy took in a couple of deep breaths just to be able to identify it.

'Phew!' he cried in disgust.

And then he tried not to breathe in so deeply after that.

The others were doing the same. Calamity as usual was overdoing it. He was holding his nose with his finger and thumb and pretending to be sick.

Mr Baxter unloaded a pile of clipboards and sheets of paper from the coach with Ms Graham's help.

The driver sprawled back in his seat and watched with a mixture of curiosity and contempt.

'Now gather round everyone,' Mr Baxter called. 'I want you all to get a clipboard and your assignment sheets. There are three sheets altogether, so make sure you get them all.'

There was chaos as the class queued up or barged in to get their equipment. It was all right for Mr Baxter. He only had to give out the clipboards, but Ms Graham had to distribute the three different sheets of the questionnaire. Some people ended up with page one and two copies of page two. Others ended up with page two and two copies of page three. There were squeals of dismay when the children found out, and they went back to try to put it right.

The driver watched with a look on his face that seemed to say he wasn't surprised.

'Now I hope no one's left anything on the coach,' Mr Baxter said when he had restored order. 'We won't be coming back here till the end of the day, so you'll need to bring your bags and picnics with you.'

There was a rush to get back on the coach.

'Teachers,' Leroy heard the driver mutter as he climbed the steps. 'They couldn't organize a booze-up in a brewery.'

Leroy gave the driver a glare and pushed down the coach to get his bag. Not that there was much left in it.

When he got off again, he found that someone had come out of the farm building and was shaking hands with Mr Baxter and Ms Graham. He was a big man with a red face and he was all smiles.

Mr Baxter turned round to them all and clapped his hands for quiet.

'Now listen, everyone,' he called. 'I want to introduce Mr Essex to you. He owns this farm, and we're very grateful to him for letting us spend the day here and for giving up his time to us.'

The teacher looked round the children expectantly, though Leroy couldn't work out what he was expecting. Nobody said or did anything.

'Aren't we,' Mr Baxter said with emphasis, and not as though it was a question.

Still nobody said or did anything.

It didn't seem to make any difference to Mr Essex. He was bowing and nodding and smiling as if they had given him a cheer or burst into applause or something.

Oh, Leroy thought, perhaps that was what Mr Baxter was waiting for. Well, it was too late now.

'First of all,' Mr Baxter went on, 'Mr Essex is going to take us to the farm office and he's going to say a few words about the farm and how it is organized. Then you'll have time to wander around and find the answers for your assignment sheets. But remember the rules. Don't chase any of the animals. Don't tread or trample on any crops. Keep to the paths. Don't leave any gates open. And don't leave any litter about, especially glass.'

Mr Baxter scanned the faces in front of him with narrowed eyes to make sure they were taking in what he was saying.

They had all heard it before. Mr Baxter had been over it with them three times already, and they'd all written it down in their books.

'Then,' Mr Baxter said, 'we meet back here at twelve o'clock and go and have our picnic. Now don't any of you be late. You'll have plenty of time in the afternoon to complete your assignment sheets.'

As they straggled along to the farm office, Calamity asked, ''Ave you got a biro?'

Leroy felt in his pocket. 'Yeah,' he said.

''Ave you got two?'

'No.'

'I'll 'ave to try an' borrow one then.'

Calamity went round begging from the others. Trust him, Leroy thought.

When he came back, Calamity said, 'None o' 'em'll loan me one, rotten lot, I'll 'ave to share with you.'

Leroy gave him a hard stare.

The farm office was small. They couldn't all get inside.

Some of them had to stand outside, crowded round the door, to try to hear what was going on from there.

Mr Essex was burbling on, but Leroy couldn't understand what he was saying. It didn't sound like any kind of English he'd ever heard. He wondered if they spoke a different language in the countryside.

Perhaps Mr Baxter realized there was some problem, because he started to repeat some of the things Mr Essex was saying, in a loud, slow voice.

'Aarh, aarh, aarh,' Mr Essex went.

'Have you got that, children?' Mr Baxter asked. 'His herd of cows has an average annual yield of 10,800 pounds of milk at 4.38 per cent butterfat. Is that right?'

Mr Essex nodded and smiled.

And then, 'Aarh, aarh, aarh,' continued Mr Essex.

'His feed works out at 2.4 pence per gallon of milk,' Mr Baxter translated.

'Aarh, aarh, aarh,' went the indefatigable Mr Essex. There was no stopping him.

'His pigs have a bacon weight of 200 pounds when they are seven to eight months old.'

And so it went on.

Leroy gave up.

He looked across and saw that Veronica Wright was scribbling down notes like mad on the paper on her clipboard. She would.

But it was too late for Leroy now. He blew out a stream of discontented air. Even if he'd written down every word that Mr Essex – or rather Mr Baxter – had said, he was sure he still wouldn't have understood what it was all about.

It was half an hour before Mr Essex finished, and only then were they free to wander around.

Leroy turned back to the yard, and Calamity tagged along.

'Hey,' Calamity cried. 'What's all these questions?'

It was as if he were seeing the assignment sheets for the first time.

Leroy let out a weary sigh. 'It's what you've got to find out. It prove we ain't been skivin'. We've been workin', not just 'avin' a day off school.'

He looked at the questions himself for the first time.

Date. That was easy.

Weather. Yes, he could write something about that.

Farmer's Name, Address, Telephone Number. Well, perhaps he could look Mr Essex up in the phone book.

Type of Farm. Were there different kinds of farms? A farm was just a farm, wasn't it?

Total acreage. He'd no idea.

Number and kind of livestock kept. How did he know? And there were still hundreds and hundreds more things to fill in.

'Come on,' he said. 'Let's go an' count the cows.' That would be something.

There was a track down the side of the farm building. It was lined by hedges, but it seemed to lead to some fields. Cows lived in fields, didn't they. They went that way.

They passed what looked like an orchard, though there was no fruit left on the trees. Perhaps it was just as well, Leroy thought.

Calamity must have noticed too because he said, 'I'm 'ungry.'

'So am I,' said Leroy.

''Ow much you got left?'

'Not much.'

'Me neither.'

They trudged on glumly. The track grew rougher and muddier. There was a squelch every time they put their feet down and a glug as they pulled them out again. Leroy had a feeling his mum wasn't going to be pleased when he got back home.

The track ended in a gate and beyond the gate was a field.

'Are they cows?' Calamity asked, pointing to the animals lazily roaming around and pulling at the grass.

'What d'you mean?' Leroy demanded snappily. 'Course they're cows.' Really, there were times . . .

'Well, they could be bulls,' Calamity pointed out.

Leroy bit back his scornful reply. Perhaps Calamity had a point.

They climbed on to the gate and studied the animals carefully.

They were white with black blotches, or black with white blotches, it was difficult to tell which. Leroy and Calamity looked especially hard at what they had underneath, by their back legs. But they didn't seem to have anything very much. Maybe they hadn't made up their minds yet what they were going to be.

'Let's say they're cows,' Leroy said in the end. 'We better count 'em.'

But it wasn't as easy as all that. The cows – or bulls – kept moving around, whisking their tails, munching the grass, licking each other. It was hard to keep up with them. Leroy lost count twice and had to start again.

'What d'you make it?' he asked at last.

'Thirty-seven,' said Calamity.

'Can't be,' said Leroy. 'I made it forty-one.'

They started again.

This time, Calamity made it thirty-nine and Leroy forty-three.

'Let's split the difference,' said Leroy. 'Call it forty-one.'

That was the number he'd first thought of. He wrote it down on the assignment sheet.

'Loan me your biro,' said Calamity.

Leroy gave him a look but he handed the biro over.

While Calamity was filling in the space, some of the cows – or whatever they were – came over to have a look at them. Close to, Leroy saw that they had big eyes with pink rims round them. They went on chewing, and strings of saliva dripped from their mouths.

Leroy leaned over and tried to pat one of the cows on the head. The cow backed away and started mooing. It sounded as if it had indigestion. The other animals took up the cry, and soon the whole herd was mooing and making a mournful noise.

'I t'ought the countryside were suppose to be quiet,' Leroy said.

As they walked back to the farm house, they passed Veronica Wright and her friend, Angie.

'Are the cows down there?' Veronica asked.

'Yeah,' said Leroy. 'I t'ink so.'

'How many are there?'

'Forty-one.'

'That ain't right,' Veronica snapped. She consulted her notes. 'Mr Essex said 'e 'ad seventy cows an' thirty-nine yearlings.'

'Well, go an' count 'em you'self,' said Leroy.

They walked on.

Leroy turned indignantly to Calamity. 'Where she get seventy cows from? I ain't seen no seventy cows. 'Ave you?'

'No,' agreed Calamity.

The faint possibility that there might be some more cows somewhere began to stir in Leroy's mind, but he managed to subdue it. Nor did he like the suggestion that reared itself that Calamity might have been right in his first count.

Until twelve o'clock they wandered around looking at the farm buildings and machinery. There were spaces on the assignment sheets that had to be filled in about these as well. It was slow work, especially when Leroy had to lend Calamity his biro all the time.

'Come on,' said Leroy, getting fed up after a while. 'It's 'bout time fo' lunch.'

They made their way back to the yard. There were others already waiting, chatting excitedly about what they had seen.

'You see the milkin' parlour?'

'What's a silo for?'

'Weren't the pigs sweet?'

'Yuck! They were so fat!'

'Yeah, one of 'em looked like Mrs Philby.'

Leroy turned to Calamity. ''Ow come we ain't seen no pigs? Where's they?' he asked accusingly.

'I dunno,' said Calamity. 'Maybe we ain't seen everythin' yet.'

That was pretty obvious, Leroy thought, but he let Calamity off. They might be able to find the pigs after lunch.

Mr Baxter and Ms Graham arrived.

'Where d'you t'ink they been all mornin'?' Leroy asked.

'I bet they been snoggin',' said Calamity.

'Never,' said Leroy scornfully. Nevertheless, he looked carefully to see whether or not Ms Graham's lipstick was smudged.

Mr Baxter and Ms Graham led the way down some paths and across some fields to a stream.

'Now stay here,' Mr Baxter warned them. 'Don't wander away. We don't want any of you getting lost. And no paddling in the water.'

The children spread themselves out and unpacked their lunches.

Calamity had his second banana. Leroy ate his apple and opened his can of orange. He had only just put it to his lips when Calamity said, 'Give us a drink.'

Leroy's mouth dropped open. He gave Calamity a hard stare, but he passed the can over.

'That's enough,' he cried before Calamity could even take a sip.

Reluctantly, Calamity passed the can back.

He gazed hungrily at the other children. 'Maybe we can scrounge somethin',' he suggested.

'You already did,' Leroy said pointedly. But it wasn't a bad idea.

They managed to get a jam sandwich, two biscuits, a piece of cheese and half a fruit tart. Lalji even let Leroy have a bit of his chapatti.

But it still didn't seem enough. Their stomachs felt empty. They sat gloomily staring at the stream and trying to subdue the pangs of hunger raging inside them.

'Where's Mr Baxter an' Miss Graham gone to?' Calamity asked after a while.

'I don' know,' said Leroy. He was getting fed up with Calamity and his endless questions. 'I t'ink they went off somewheres. Fo' a walk.'

'I bet they've gone so's they can be alone,' said Calamity. He winked suggestively. 'Let's go an' see.'

Leroy didn't think much of the idea, but it might take his mind off his empty stomach.

'OK.'

They followed the stream for a bit and then came to a place where the stream dipped down or the ground rose, they couldn't tell which. They struggled up this incline, grabbing tufts of grass to help them.

Calamity was in front. He suddenly ducked down and waved back at Leroy warningly. Then he grinned and made violent pointing gestures ahead.

Leroy wondered if he had gone mad.

He pulled himself up to where Calamity was. They both lay on the ground, inched forward and peered over.

Mr Baxter and Ms Graham were sitting on the grass in a hollow with the stream bubbling away at their feet.

Calamity grinned at Leroy and nodded his head triumphantly.

Leroy examined the teachers again. They were sitting quite close, but they weren't touching. He couldn't see anything special to get excited about. It was just Calamity overworking his imagination again.

Calamity was pushing forward, craning his neck in his eagerness to see more when Ms Graham suddenly looked round. She must have sensed something. Calamity and Leroy didn't have time to duck.

She jumped to her feet and shouted at them. 'What are you boys doing there?' She sounded really cross.

Mr Baxter was standing up now too. Calamity and Leroy had no option. They pulled themselves up to their feet and tried to look innocent.

'I thought I told you to stay in the picnic area,' said Mr Baxter. 'Not to wander around. What are you up to?'

'Nothin',' said Calamity.

'We was just goin' fo' a walk,' said Leroy.

'Well, you can just go for a walk back where you came from,' snapped Ms Graham.

'And I'll have something to say to you both when I get back,' warned Mr Baxter.

Leroy and Calamity turned and went.

Leroy had had enough. That was it. He was fed up with Calamity getting him into trouble. Fed up with Calamity borrowing his biro all the time. Fed up with Calamity asking him questions he couldn't answer. Fed up with feeling hungry. Fed up with the countryside. He hadn't wanted to come in the first place.

When they got back to the others, Calamity stopped, but Leroy went on walking.

'Hey,' Calamity called. 'Where you goin'? Mr Baxter said we was to come back 'ere.'

Leroy ignored him. He just walked on.

Calamity called again. Still, Leroy didn't answer. He half expected Calamity to come running after him, but he didn't.

'Good,' Leroy muttered to himself. 'Then maybe I won' get in no more trouble.'

He was dimly aware he was already in trouble for not doing what Mr Baxter had told him to do. But he didn't care. He marched on purposefully along the path that followed the stream. He passed field after field. It was only after some time that he began to wonder if he would be able to find his way back.

He halted to consider his position. It wasn't too difficult. He only had to go back the way he had come, along the stream, to the picnic place, and then go up from there, and he would reach the farm.

Where he had stopped there was a fence with a stile in it. Leroy climbed it. Well, since he was there, he might as well explore.

By now, the sun had come out and it was quite hot for the time of year. As he tramped up the footpath by the side of the

field, Leroy felt his face break out in sweat. He must have been walking too fast. He slowed down.

The field stretched away on his left. Something had been planted in long rows, and the fresh green shoots were already showing. It seemed a funny time to Leroy to be planting things with the winter ahead, but he supposed the farmer knew what he was doing.

He came to another stile and clambered over it. This field was just grass. It seemed a bit of a waste.

When he mounted the next stile, he paused. The ground must have risen because from his vantage point he had a clear view over the fields and hedgerows for what seemed like miles and miles. The green and brown patchwork quilt of the countryside stretched all around him. Trees hid the view in some directions, but not enough to prevent a sense of a vast panorama unfolding before him.

Leroy turned his head full circle to take it all in. He could have been in the middle of nowhere. Not another human being was in sight. Just fields spreading out before him and trees rising up to the sky that arched wide above him.

'Wow!' Leroy exclaimed aloud. So this was what the countryside was about.

Then his eye caught sight of something in the field immediately in front of him. Horses. There were five of them at the far end. One was white, and the others were dark brown. They were standing still, facing each other, occasionally tossing their heads, as though having a chat.

And then suddenly, for no reason at all that Leroy could see, they kicked their heels up in the air and began chasing each other round the field. Leroy laughed as he watched them. It was like children playing games. They trotted round and round, butting each other and drawing back, galloping madly, shaking their manes and looking over their shoulders.

For a moment, Leroy wondered what it would be like to climb on to the back of one of them, cling to the neck and go charging round the field. But, big though he was, he didn't think he would be able to reach up and get his leg over.

It was a nice idea though.

The horses seemed to have stopped their game. They were just ambling about now, rather aimlessly. And then one of them must have noticed Leroy because they came trooping over towards the stile.

Leroy almost dropped off backwards, but he recovered his balance and stayed where he was. Soon the horses were all around him, nuzzling him, sniffing at him.

He stretched out his hand to stroke them on the foreheads. How hard their heads felt!

He knocked with his fist, but not too forcefully. The horses seemed to like it. Their big eyes were turned on him — curious, not exactly friendly, but not hostile either. It was more a sort of calm acceptance.

And then, without warning, the horses drew back, reared up and went galloping round the field again. Leroy nearly fell off the stile with delight.

'What are you doing here?'

Once more Leroy nearly fell off the stile, this time from shock.

He swung round and saw a girl standing behind him.

'What are you doing here?' she repeated.

Leroy scrambled down from the stile and stood to face her.

The girl was a couple of years older than he was, he guessed, but about the same height. Her long fair hair was pulled to the back in a pony tail. She was wearing a white shirt and those tight trousers people wore for riding.

'I were just lookin',' he explained.

Her voice hadn't been particularly angry, but there was no point in taking chances.

'This is private property,' the girl went on.

But again, she didn't sound too put out about finding someone trespassing. In fact, she was staring at Leroy in a way that he couldn't explain. It was embarrassing really. She was wide-eyed and she was gazing at him as if he were a visitor from outer space.

'Is them yours, then?' he asked, nodding at the horses, and hoping this would distract her attention from him.

'Oh, yes,' the girl said, coming out of her trance to give the horses a glance. 'But I'm not allowed to ride them at the moment. You see, I've been ill, and the doctor says I've got to be careful for a while.'

The skin of her face was certainly very pale.

'I guess you like ridin',' Leroy said, feeling a bit easier now.

'Oh, yes,' the girl said with enthusiasm. 'I ride every day when I'm not at school.'

The mention of the word must have reminded her because she went on, 'I'm going back to school tomorrow. Mummy's taking me.'

Her voice sounded strange to Leroy. Like somebody talking posh on television. But she seemed friendly enough now.

'Do they 'ave names?' he asked.

'Yes. There's Topsy and Trudy and Flash and Bingo and Penelope.'

Leroy glanced at the horses and wondered which was which. But there was no way of telling.

He turned back to the girl. She was gazing at him in that embarrassing way again. He tried desperately to think of something else to say, but he couldn't.

Then she just came out with it.

'I've got a black baby,' she said proudly.

Leroy's mouth dropped open as he swung round to stare at her. He was thinking wildly. How come? She wasn't old enough, was she? And how could it be black?

But he pretended to be cool and a man of the world.

'Oh yeah,' he said as casually as he could. 'That's good.' It was the best he could manage.

'Yes,' the girl continued, not noticing his surprise. 'We pay eight pounds a month for him. His name's Samuel. He's five.'

Leroy stared in amazement in spite of himself. How was it possible? She only looked thirteen now, at the most. How could she have had a baby when she was eight? And what was this about paying for him? Eight pounds a month wouldn't go far.

'He lives in Sierra Leone,' the girl went on. 'When he's old enough, he'll write me letters and tell me how he's getting on.'

Leroy was still uncertain. Where was Sierra Leone?

'Of course, he's not really my baby. But I like to think of him like that. We just sponsor him.'

It began to be clear. Leroy had heard of things like that. Churches ran sponsorship schemes, didn't they? To help children in need get an education and have enough to eat.

'I've got a photograph,' the girl said. 'Would you like to see it?'

'Wouldn't mind,' Leroy said. There was nothing to be lost by it.

'Come up to the house then.'

'All right.'

The girl climbed over the stile into the field with the horses, and Leroy followed. The horses came bounding over to see her, and she made a fuss of them, stroking their manes and patting their broad solid backs and calling them by their names. They were very tame and mild. They let Leroy stroke them as well. The hair on their manes was soft and silky, but on their backs it was quite hard and stubbly like a toothbrush.

Reluctantly, the girl left the horses and she and Leroy moved along the footpath. They were silent for a while. And then the girl suddenly turned to him and asked, 'Are you from Africa?'

'No, London,' Leroy replied.

'Oh,' the girl said. She sounded disappointed.

She noticed the clipboard he was still carrying.

'What's that?' she asked.

Leroy explained about the visit to the farm and about how they had to write down things about it.

'Oh, that's Rocksby Farm,' the girl said. 'It's next-door to us.'

Then she thought. 'You could put the horses down, couldn't you?'

'Yeah,' Leroy agreed. 'I could.'

And he did just that. It would help fill some of the empty spaces on the assignment sheets.

They came to a gate this time. It was open. They passed through into what seemed to be more of a park than a field. The grass was much shorter and neater than it had been before. A pebbled path curved among trees and bushes. Leroy hoped he would be able to find his way back to the farm.

Then there was suddenly a huge lawn spreading in front of them like a lake, and on the furthest edge of it stood a house. Leroy had never seen such a big house. It was four storeys high with tall windows, and there must have been ten or twelve windows on each floor. The front door stuck out in the middle and had pillars round it. It was a mansion.

'D'you live 'ere?' Leroy asked.

'Yes.'

'Who else live 'ere?'

'Well, there's Mummy and Dadddy and Nanny, and Dick and Sally, though Dick and Sally only come in during the day. And there's Charles, of course, but he's away at school at the moment.'

Leroy couldn't believe it. That great house for just seven people, and half of them weren't there most of the time! He had a feeling he shouldn't be there either.

A piercing scream suddenly cut through the still air. Leroy nearly jumped out of his skin.

'What were that?' he cried.

'Oh, it's just the peacock,' the girl told him without much interest.

She pointed to the far edge of the lawn where it was shaded by some tall trees. That must have been why Leroy hadn't noticed it before. A big bird was strutting up and down. It looked as if it were in a bad temper. There were two other birds nearby, slightly smaller. They didn't seem to be paying much attention to the peacock.

'I don't like them much,' the girl said. 'They're not very friendly and they peck at you. But Daddy wanted them.'

The peacock had emerged from the shadows now and was in full sunlight. Its tail opened in a wide fan of dazzling irridescent blues and greens. Leroy gaped at it.

'He is beautiful, though,' the girl said.

Leroy had to agree.

'He keeps dropping his tail feathers on the lawn,' the girl went on. 'I've got some in my room.'

Then she had a sudden thought. 'Would you like one?'

Leroy nodded his head enthusiastically.

'Right,' said the girl. 'I'll give you one. And you can put *peacock* down on your list. And *peahens*.'

Leroy hastily scribbled them down.

They were almost at the front door by now.

'By the way,' the girl said, 'my name's Emma Houghton. What's yours?'

Leroy dragged his eyes away from the peacock and told her.

'Just in case Mummy asks,' Emma explained.

She pushed open the door and went in. Leroy was amazed it hadn't been locked. They never dared leave their door open on the estate.

Inside, the house seemed to be all wood and polish. The entrance hall was ten times as big as his living room back home. The floors and panelled walls glowed. There were rugs on the floors and dark pictures on the walls. A wide staircase rose up on one side.

'Mummy,' Emma called out. 'I've brought a friend.'

Her boots clattered on the floor as she strode towards a door. Leroy followed her apprehensively. He wondered what he was letting himself in for. He noticed that his boots were muddy, but the rugs looked too good to wipe them on, and anyway, there wasn't time. The door was open and Emma was beckoning to him.

Emma's mother stood up as he entered. It was just as well

she did, or he might have missed her, the room was so big
and bright with sunlight, and full of cabinets and tables and
comfortable-looking flowery armchairs and sofas.

'This is Leroy,' Emma announced.

Emma's mother remained where she was for a moment.
She was tall and thin and wearing a summery dress. Leroy
had a second or two of worry. He wasn't sure how she was
going to react to his unexpected appearance. His own mum
would probably have had something to say if it had been the
other way round and he had suddenly arrived with Emma.

But he needn't have worried. Mrs Houghton didn't bat an
eyelid. She smiled with a flash of very white teeth and strode
towards Leroy with an outstretched hand.

'Hello, Leroy,' she said as she squeezed his hand. Her
voice was loud and clear as if she were used to making
speeches. She had a good grip too – as strong as a man's.

'He's visiting Rocksby Farm,' Emma explained. 'Mr
Essex.'

Well, Leroy thought, it was more or less correct.

'Is he now?' said Mrs Houghton, her face filling with
interest. 'Isn't that nice? How kind of you to drop in. Do sit
down.'

Leroy didn't know where to sit. There was such a choice.
In the end, he sat on one of the sofas facing the huge
fireplace. Emma settled down beside him, and Mrs Houghton lowered herself on to one of the armchairs.

'What school do you go to?' Mrs Houghton asked.

Leroy told her.

Mrs Houghton thought for a moment and then shook her
head. 'I don't know it.'

Leroy didn't see any reason why she should.

'Are you staying at the farm long?'

'Only till this afternoon,' Leroy said.

'Oh, what a pity Emma didn't meet you earlier. You could
have been company for her. She's been ill, you know. But
never mind. Next time you're down you must let us know
and come and see us.'

Mrs Houghton went on asking questions. She seemed to be genuinely interested in what Leroy had to say. Or else she was used to being polite to people.

Then she said, 'I must tear myself away, pleasant though it is to sit here and chat. I have work to do.'

Leroy couldn't imagine what kind of work. He couldn't see her scrubbing the floors.

Mrs Houghton stood up. 'I'll ask Sally to make some orange juice, shall I?'

'Oh super, Mum,' Emma cried.

Mrs Houghton stretched out her hand again and shook Leroy's.

'I look forward to seeing you the next time you're down,' she said.

Leroy wasn't sure, but she seemed to mean it. And she hadn't even noticed his muddy boots. Or if she had she'd been too nice to say anything.

When they were alone, Leroy and Emma talked about their school and friends. He told her about Calamity and Veronica Wright and Mr Baxter. She told him about prep and violin lessons and midnight feasts. It sounded quite fun, but Leroy thought his school was better. He didn't fancy the idea of living away from home.

When the orange juice arrived, it had cubes of ice in it, and it was freshly squeezed. It was solid with fruit. There was a cake too which Sally said she'd just made. It was still slightly warm, sponge cake with jam and cream in the middle. Leroy had two slices. He wanted to have a third, but Emma had only had two slices so he thought it was polite to refuse. But he was sorely tempted to have another slice. It was so light it melted in the mouth.

Suddenly he remembered the time. It was nearly three o'clock. What if the coach left without him?

'I better be goin',' he said, and hurriedly got to his feet.

'Oh, must you?' Emma cried, and then she remembered what he was doing in this part of the world. 'Yes, I suppose you must. Just a minute. I'll get the peacock feather for you.

Oh, and I nearly forgot. There's the photograph I was going to show you.'

While she was out of the room, Leroy gazed around him. It sure would be nice to live in a house like this, he thought. There was so much of it.

When she came back, Emma was holding two peacock's feathers. She handed them to Leroy. 'I can always get some more,' she said.

Leroy took them and marvelled at them. The eyes seemed to be alive, glowing at him. The colours gleamed emerald and dark blue like colours under the sea.

'T'anks,' he mumbled, but it didn't seem enough.

"And this is Samuel,' Emma said proudly, holding out a photograph.

Leroy took it and studied the black face that peered up at him. He almost laughed. With its squinty eyes and crooked grin it was the spitting image of Tommy Walker who lived next-door. He was about five.

But he managed to restrain himself. 'Very nice,' he mumbled as he handed it back.

He was getting more and more anxious about the time. Not only that, but there was the problem of finding his way back as well.

'I better be goin',' he said again.

But still Emma seemed reluctant to lose him. There was a rather sad expression on her pale face, and she was looking undecided.

Then she blurted it out. 'Will you write to me?' she asked.

She hurried on. 'Just till Samuel is old enough to write.'

Leroy wasn't so sure, but he felt he couldn't very well refuse.

'Well, yeah,' he said. 'OK.'

Emma went to a cabinet and took a sheet of notepaper out of a drawer. She folded it in half and tore it across. She handed the top half to Leroy. There was a big crest on it and the address was heavily embossed.

'And what's your address?' Emma asked.

Leroy told her, and she wrote it down on the other half of the sheet of notepaper.

By now, Leroy was getting desperate.

'I ain't sure 'ow I'm gonna get back to the farm,' he moaned.

'But that's easy,' said Emma. 'You just have to go up to the road, turn right, and it's the next turning you come to.'

So that was all right. But he would still have to hurry.

Emma walked with him up the drive to the road. There were huge wrought-iron gates, towering at least twice as tall as they were above them. Emma pushed one of them open just wide enough for Leroy to squeeze through. He danced from foot to foot, wondering how to get away.

'T'anks for the feathers,' he said at last. 'An' the cake an' orange juice an' everyt'in'.'

'Not at all,' said Emma. 'You will write, won't you?'

'Well, yeah, OK.'

And then he was off, pounding along the road.

'Goodbye,' Emma called after him.

He turned for a moment to wave to her, but continued running backwards down the road.

Heaven knew what Mr Baxter was going to say. That was, if he was still there. If it took the coach an hour to get there, how long would it take Leroy to walk home? Days probably, if his feet could stand it, and he could find the way. The sinking feeling in his stomach began to grow heavier and heavier.

But his head felt quite light. He chuckled and then laughed out loud. Get him. Hobnobbing with the aristocrats. He'd thought people like that would have been too toffee-nosed to speak to him. Most of them were probably. But these two had been all right. Wait till he told the others.

But then his pace slackened for a moment as he thought about it. Perhaps it would be better not to tell them. Perhaps they wouldn't understand.

And the peacock feathers waving in his hand? What about them? If the rest of them saw them, they'd only want them or mess about and break them. But where could he hide them?

They wouldn't go in his bag.

Leroy stopped. He put down his bag and his clipboard. He took one of the feathers and slipped the end into the top of his sweater. He reached up under the sweater and drew the feather down carefully. It tickled his cheek. He did the same with the other one. They were safely concealed now. They might get a bit damaged, but at least no one would know they were there.

He picked up his bag and clipboard and went swinging along the road again.

He soon came to the turning Emma had mentioned and the sign 'Rocksby Farm'. He broke into a run.

The coach was still there. A group of children stood around it. Mr Baxter was there as well, and Ms Graham. Leroy slowed down, changing his trot into a leisurely stroll. There was no point in wasting energy.

When the children saw him, they set up a cheer. But Mr Baxter wasn't smiling. Neither was Ms Graham. They were furious. Leroy could tell.

'Where d'you think you've been?' Mr Baxter demanded. 'We've been waiting half an hour for you.'

'I were lost,' Leroy protested. It was the first thing that came into his head.

But nobody showed any sympathy.

'No consideration for anybody,' Ms Graham snapped.

'Keeping us all waiting,' Mr Baxter fumed.

Leroy scowled at them glumly. They were taking all the pleasure out of the day.

'Well, we'd better get on the coach now,' said Mr Baxter. 'But I'll have something to say to you later. Give me your clipboard.'

Leroy handed it to him and began to walk towards the coach.

'Wait a minute,' Mr Baxter called.

Leroy turned round. Mr Baxter was skimming through the sheets.

'You've done hardly any of the questions.'

'I were lost, I told you,' Leroy maintained. 'I 'ad to spend all my time tryin' to find where I were.'

But Mr Baxter wasn't listening. Something had caught his eye.

'What's this?' he demanded. 'Horses. Mr Essex doesn't have any horses.'

'Well, I seen 'em,' said Leroy stubbornly.

'And . . . and . . .' Mr Baxter suddenly exploded. 'Peacocks!'

Mr Baxter's scream was one the peacock itself would have envied.

Leroy put his head up and stuck his chin out. 'Yeah.'

'You've been making it all up,' Mr Baxter yelled angrily.

'No, I ain't,' cried Leroy. He was getting angry too.

He reached under the hem of his sweater and drew out one of the feathers with a flourish. The feather quivered in the air, its colours gleaming and glowing.

Mr Baxter blinked and stared at it. There were oohs and gasps from the children.

'But it's lovely,' cried Ms Graham.

'Can I 'ave it?' Veronica Wright asked, her eyes fixed on it enviously.

Leroy had known that was what would happen.

He turned to Ms Graham. 'Would you like it, miss?'

Ms Graham's face flushed with pleasure. 'That is kind of you, Leroy. Are you sure?'

Leroy nodded his head and held the feather out.

Ms Graham took it and began to stroke it gently. 'Thank you, Leroy.'

Mr Baxter cleared his throat. 'Come along, everybody,' he barked. 'On the coach. Or we'll never get home today.'

But Leroy had a feeling the form teacher wasn't going to have quite so much to say to him later as he had planned.

As he climbed on to the coach, Leroy's eyes met those of the driver who was sitting at the wheel, tight-lipped and hard faced.

'I got a schedule to keep,' the driver muttered, furious.

Leroy held his gaze for a moment without blinking. As he moved down the coach, he wondered if it meant the same as having a family to keep.

Calamity had bagged a place for him.

'Where you been?' he demanded grumpily.

'Like I told Mr Baxter,' Leroy said, 'I got lost.'

He wasn't sure he wanted to tell even Calamity about it. And besides, after what had happened, he wasn't sure he even wanted to talk to him.

It was quiet on the journey home. The children seemed to be worn out by their exertions and all the country air.

The first thing Mum said as Leroy burst through the door was, 'Phew!' She bent down to sniff at his sweater. 'You can tell you been in the country!'

Then she noticed his boots. 'Look at the state o' 'em. Get 'em off before you takes another step.'

Leroy crouched down and began to untie the laces.

'An' you make sure you cleans 'em before you goes to bed,' Mum warned.

When Leroy produced the peacock feather and gave it to Paulette, she was delighted with it.

'So you did bring me a present,' she cried. She gazed at it for ages, scarcely daring to touch it. 'It's so beautiful,' she murmured. Her voice was as full of wonder as her eyes. She danced round with it, tickling everyone under the chin.

Later that evening, Leroy discovered the folded ·piece of notepaper in his pocket. He took it out and looked at the fancy crest and the address. Houghton Hall. Imagine having a house named after you! He ran his fingers over the lettering. The embossing was so thick a blind person could have read it.

He thought over the day. Perhaps the countryside wasn't so bad after all. There was that view from the top of the stile. The horses. The peacock feather. Houghton Hall. Emma and her mother.

'I t'inks maybe I adopts a white baby,' he mused.

It was a nice idea, though at the back of his mind he knew he probably wouldn't.

He must have said it out loud because when he glanced up, he saw Mum giving him an odd look.

Lost and Found

Mr Baxter wasn't pleased with Leroy. But then, Leroy wasn't very pleased with Mr Baxter.

The form teacher had told Leroy to stay behind after school because there were one or two things he wanted to talk to him about. Leroy could guess what they were. It had been a bad day. It was one of those days when everything seemed to go wrong. Somehow, he kept getting into trouble. Ms Graham had told him off for talking in class. He had forgotten to bring his exercise books for maths. He was late for his geography lesson.

Leroy was sure it had all got back to Mr Baxter. That was the way teachers were. They always told on you. You'd have thought they'd have something more interesting to talk about. But no.

And that was what Mr Baxter wanted to see him about. Leroy was sure of it.

He watched gloomily as the rest of the class left. Calamity waved his head from side to side with a stupid grin on it. Leroy stuck his tongue out at him. Veronica Wright tutted with disapproval. Leroy stared her out.

Now there were just Leroy and Mr Baxter.

Sitting at his desk in the front row, Leroy watched Mr Baxter gathering his books and papers together. He hadn't even started talking to him yet. It would take hours at this rate.

Leroy had a suspicion Mr Baxter was doing it on purpose, keeping him waiting, wasting his time. It wasn't fair. None of it was fair. Just because he'd done a few things wrong. There'd been weeks when he'd been perfect, not a foot out of place. But did Mr Baxter notice that? Oh no. It was only when he did something wrong that Mr Baxter paid any attention.

But that wasn't what was really worrying Leroy. He could put up with that if he had to.

No, it was Paulette. He had to pick her up from school. And if he was late, Paulette wouldn't know what had happened to him, and she wouldn't know what to do.

'You ain't suppose to keep me in wit'out you gives me twenty-four hours' notice,' Leroy told Mr Baxter. 'It's a rule.'

Mr Baxter went on shuffling his papers.

'I know that, Leroy,' he said quietly. 'But it's a matter of interpretation. I'm not keeping you in. I just want to have a little talk.'

'Seem the same t'ing to me,' Leroy grumbled.

'Not at all,' said Mr Baxter. 'As I said, it's all a matter of interpretation.'

Leroy's eyes narrowed as he brooded over it. Wasn't that just like teachers again? If they couldn't have it one way, they'd have it another.

Leroy went back to the attack.

'I've got to collect my sister from school,' he said. 'If you keeps me in, I'll be late, an' she'll be all worried.'

'But I'm not keeping you in,' Mr Baxter pointed out calmly. 'I just told you that. I just want to have a little talk with you. I'm sure your sister will wait.'

'Oh no she won't,' Leroy cried.

'Oh yes she will,' Mr Baxter assured him.

'She won't.'

'She will.'

Leroy paused. Mr Baxter was giving a good performance of staying cool and reasonable. It was puzzling. But Leroy knew the teacher couldn't keep it up for long. He was bound to crack.

Leroy returned to the attack.

'But I've got to pick her up, sir,' he pleaded. 'My mum told me to. An' if I don', my mum'll be all worried too.'

'I'm sure your mother will understand,' said Mr Baxter. 'If you explain it properly.'

'Oh no she won't,' Leroy cried. 'You don' know my mum.'

'Oh yes she will,' returned Mr Baxter.

'Oh no she won't.'

'Oh yes she . . .'

Mr Baxter stopped. He closed his mouth firmly. He made an effort to restrain himself.

'Of course,' he said, 'the longer we argue about that, the longer it will be before we can talk about what I want to talk about, and the later you will be.'

Leroy eventually worked out what Mr Baxter meant. He was not impressed. It only made him feel more worried and more annoyed. If that was logic, then he had his own logic. What was more important? What his mum said or what a teacher said? He knew the answer to that one.

He shoved his chair back and stood up.

'I've got to collect my sister,' he said stubbornly.

And he walked out of the room.

'Come back this minute,' Mr Baxter yelled.

At last he'd cracked. Leroy knew he would. But he didn't have time to worry about the teacher's temper. He belted along the corridor and down the stairs two at a time.

Of course, he'd be in worse trouble next time he saw Mr Baxter. He'd probably get a detention. It would be the first one he'd had. But he couldn't help that. He had his job to do, and he had to do it. His duty to his family was much more important than doing what the teacher said.

As he trotted down the drive, he checked his watch. He was a quarter of an hour late. He wasn't really worried. In spite of what he'd told Mr Baxter, he knew Paulette would wait for him. She always did.

There was a crowd of parents and children standing on the pavement outside the junior school. Leroy joined them. As he looked around, the thought crossed his mind that maybe there weren't as many people there as usual, but he didn't let that bother him. There was still plenty of time.

Children were still dawdling in the playground and trooping out of the school building.

But then the people began to drift away. Soon only one or two remained. There was still no sign of Paulette. Leroy began to feel alarmed. He couldn't have missed her, could he? She wouldn't have gone off on her own, would she?

He took a few steps down the drive towards the school, and then stopped. What was he going to do? If he went home without Paulette, all hell would break loose.

And it was getting dark, too.

As he dithered about what to do next, Mr Duffy appeared at the entrance, having a last look round to make sure everything was all right.

Should he ask Mr Duffy, Leroy wondered. At least he would know whether Paulette was still in the building. But what would Mr Duffy say if he knew Leroy had been late and hadn't collected Paulette as he was supposed to?

Leroy turned and began to retrace his steps, huddling his head into his shoulders, and trying to look inconspicuous. But he was out of luck. Mr Duffy spotted him.

'Hey, Leroy!' the headmaster called.

There was nothing for it but to stop.

'How are you getting on at the big school?' Mr Duffy asked as he came up to him. 'Are you in the football team yet? How many goals have you scored?'

Leroy answered as briefly as he could without being rude, and listened as the headmaster went into an endless speech about the good old days and what it was like when Leroy had been in the team. Leroy felt his eyes begin to glaze over. Mr Duffy certainly seemed to like the sound of his own voice.

Then Mr Duffy must have noticed that Leroy was alone.

'Where's Paulette?' he asked.

Leroy swallowed and thought quickly.

'She's probably waitin' up the road,' he said. 'By the ice-cream van.'

Well, it wasn't exactly a lie. It might even be true.

'I won't keep you then,' said Mr Duffy, 'or your mum'll be

Family Butchers
ROYAL
BOOKMAKERS

worrying where you are.'

But he went on for another five minutes before Leroy was finally able to get away.

Mum would be worrying all right, Leroy thought as he hurried along the pavement. What he wouldn't do to Mr Baxter for bringing about all this trouble!

The ice-cream van was still there, but Paulette wasn't. There was nobody there at all. As he padded past, Leroy gazed longingly at the towers of cones. No, he told himself, this was no time for self-indulgence. He quickened his stride.

He had decided that if he went fast and followed the normal route home, he might catch up with Paulette on the way. Then they could arrive at the flat together, and no one would be any the wiser. It would also save Paulette from getting into trouble. Mum was always warning her not to come home by herself.

Then another idea struck. Leroy tripped up and came to a halt as the horror of it sank in. Supposing Paulette hadn't set off for home on her own. Supposing she'd been kidnapped.

His mind was in a whirl. That wasn't possible, was it? Such things couldn't happen. And yet, he'd seen programmes about it on television. People did get kidnapped.

He really was in for it if that turned out to be true. And then there was Paulette. What about her? It was too awful to think about. Leroy gulped and hurried on.

The shopping centre was crowded with pupils waiting to catch their buses home. At least, that was their excuse. They used to wait there for hours, letting buses go by, so they could talk and mess about. Leroy knew his brother was almost always there, hanging about with his mates and chatting up the girls.

As he threaded his way through the mob, Leroy wondered what he would say if he bumped into Floyd. He kept his eyes skinned just in case.

But he wasn't sharp enough. He didn't see Floyd until someone pounced on him from behind and grabbed him round the shoulders. Leroy twisted round and found himself staring into Floyd's grinning face. He struggled free.

'What you doin' 'ere?' Floyd asked.

'I'm goin' 'ome,' Leroy growled as if Floyd had asked him a stupid question.

He made to go on, but his brother took hold of his arm.

'Where's Paulette?' he asked.

'She's round 'ere somewheres,' Leroy replied casually.

Well, it was near enough the truth. She had to be round there somewhere. Unless she'd been kidnapped.

'You better 'urry,' Floyd said, and he broke into a grin again. 'Else Mum gonna give you lashes.'

Leroy kissed his teeth. He couldn't see there was anything to laugh about.

'Hey, Floyd,' someone called. 'There's Diane.'

Floyd was off like a shot. He didn't even bother to say goodbye.

Not that Leroy minded. He breathed out a sigh of relief and pushed on towards home.

He pounded up the stairs of the flats to the fifth floor. But once he got there, he stopped. He needed to get his breath back. But he needed to think as well.

He stared along the walkway to where his front door was. There was no one in sight. There had been no sign of Paulette on the way. He had to decide what to do next.

Perhaps Paulette was already home. Safe inside the flat. But he didn't know, and he couldn't go and find out. Because either way he would be for the high jump. If she was there, he would get it for letting her come home on her own. If she wasn't there, he would get it for losing her.

Heads, tails, he just couldn't win. He was in the same kind of fix he'd been in with Mr Baxter.

He went on racking his brains, but no matter how hard he tried, no solution presented itself. He gazed over the parapet down at the ground, far below him. Paulette could be anywhere.

Then, out of the corner of his eye, he noticed someone coming towards him along the walkway. It was Mrs

Macauley with a shopping bag. She was always in and out. She knew everything that went on in the flats. Perhaps he could ask her.

''Ello, Leroy,' Mrs Macauley said with a smile. ''Ow's school?'

'OK,' Leroy replied. Then he summoned up his courage and asked, ''Ave you seen Paulette?'

'Why? She playin' 'ide an' seek?'

'Sort of.'

Well, it was true in a way.

'Ooh, the little rascal,' cried Mrs Macauley. 'I can't 'elp you there, Leroy. There's lots o' places she could 'ide in round 'ere.'

Then she dismissed the problem from her mind and got back to more serious matters. 'Are the lifts workin'?' she asked.

'No.'

'My poor legs. Well, I'll just 'ave to take 'em one at a time.'

She laughed as if she'd made a joke and trotted off, waving her empty shopping bag from side to side.

Leroy scowled after her. A fat lot of use she'd been. He still didn't know if Paulette was home or not. And he still couldn't face going home himself in case she wasn't.

He waited a while to give Mrs Macauley time to get clear and then clumped down the stairs again.

Maybe Paulette *was* playing hide and seek. Well, not that exactly. But maybe she had dawdled somewhere on the way home, and Leroy had simply missed seeing her. The only thing to do was to follow the road back to school and search every inch of the way, though that wasn't going to do much good if she'd been kidnapped. Leroy thrust the idea away. It didn't bear thinking about.

Before setting off along the road, he looked in the car park. A gang of older boys was playing football there, but they wouldn't know where Paulette was. They wouldn't have been interested in her.

He stepped out along the road, eyes alert for any trace of his sister. When he came to a side street, he stopped and scanned its full length for any tell-tale signs before going on. He had a feeling it was all going to be a waste of time, but what else could he do?

He had almost reached the shopping centre when he saw a figure approaching that filled him with a mixture of alarm and hope. It was a policeman.

As the man drew nearer and nearer, Leroy debated with himself. Should he or shouldn't he? Well, that was what policemen were for, wasn't it, he decided in the end.

The policeman was coming level. He was about to pass. It was now or never.

'Excuse me,' Leroy stammered.

The policeman stopped and examined Leroy coolly. Leroy was surprised that he came up to the policeman's shoulders. Either policemen were getting smaller or he was getting bigger.

'It's my sister,' Leroy went on. ''Ave you seen 'er?'

'Maybe I have, maybe I haven't,' the policeman replied cautiously. 'What does she look like?'

What did she look like, Leroy wondered. He was sure he would recognize her again when he saw her, but he couldn't think how to describe her.

'Well, she's eight,' he began.

'What else?'

'She's about this high.' He stuck his hand out level with his chest. 'An' she 'as 'er 'air done up in plaits.'

'I see,' said the policeman slowly. 'That shouldn't be any problem.'

Leroy was sure he was giving him a funny look.

'And what was she wearing?' was the policeman's next question.

Leroy's mind went a blank. He hadn't the foggiest idea. He never noticed what clothes Paulette was wearing. Then he suddenly remembered. She would be wearing her navy-blue raincoat. He told the policeman.

'A navy-blue raincoat,' the policeman repeated. 'She'll stick out like a sore thumb wearing that, and no mistake.'

Leroy began to wonder if the policeman was taking him seriously.

'And when did you last see your sister?' the policeman asked.

'This morning,' Leroy told him. 'On the way to school. But I were supposed to meet 'er after school an' she weren't there. That were 'bout an hour ago.'

Leroy could feel that the policeman was losing interest in him. He could tell by the way he spoke and the look on his face. He was getting ready to move on.

'But she might 'ave been kidnapped,' Leroy burst out.

The policeman was eyeing him closely.

'Now listen, son,' he said quietly. 'My advice to you is to go home and see if your sister is there. And if she isn't, I suggest you tell your mum or your dad to give me a ring at the station. Right then, I'll be on my way. I've got other things to do.'

Leroy watched as the policeman strolled down the street.

He was fuming about the policeman's behaviour. What else did they have to do? As far as Leroy could see, the policeman was only going for a walk. Here was Paulette practically kidnapped, and the police just didn't care. Floyd was right. The police were useless.

And then he felt his eyes begin to fill with tears. What was he going to do now? How could he go home, like the policeman said? If Paulette was there, he'd get a real telling off. And if she wasn't . . .

It was all Mr Baxter's fault.

''Ello, Leroy.'

Leroy blinked back his tears and swung round. While he'd been lost in his troubles, Veronica Wright had crept up on him.

'Hi,' he muttered. But he wasn't particularly pleased to see her. She was always getting in the way. How could he think clearly and work out what to do next with her there? She was bound to go on jabbering non-stop. She always did. He groaned inwardly as she began.

'I've just been to the shop to get some more lemonade,' she said, holding up the bag she was carrying.

'It's for Nicole's birthday party. They've run out already. They don't 'alf drink a lot. We thought there'd be plenty for everyone, but it just all went. You'd think they was dyin' o' thirst the way they guzzled it down.'

Leroy was wondering how to get away. He still had the shopping centre to search.

'But it's a very nice party. Everyone's 'avin' so much fun. There's lots to eat an' balloons an' fancy 'ats an' games. They was just startin' the disco when I left to get the lemonade. Oh, they do look funny, those little ones, wrigglin' about an' pretendin' they're dancin'. It makes me laugh just to look at 'em.'

'Oh yeah?' said Leroy. 'I gotta be . . . '

But Veronica rushed on.

'Nicole lives next door to me. I told 'er mum I'd give 'er a 'and. With the organizin' an' gettin' things ready an' things like that. Well, you can't expect Nicole to be much use at that sort of thing. She's only eight. An' she wanted all 'er friends to come, an' there was so much to do. Mrs Ross was ever so grateful.'

Leroy was feeling battered. Why did girls have to go twittering on so much. He'd never find Paulette at this rate.

'I better . . . ' he began.

But Veronica didn't even notice.

She went on to tell Leroy about all the preparations, what she'd had to buy, what she'd made, how she'd helped with the decorations.

Then she gave a sudden yelp.

'Oh dear. I don't know why I'm standin' 'ere talkin' when they're waitin' for this lemonade. All those little kids will be parched, what with all that dancin' an' jumpin' about. You should 'ave stopped me.'

Leroy tried hard to restrain himself. But suddenly something began to stir in his brain.

'Birthday party?' he asked.

'Yes,' said Veronica.

'Eight-year-olds?'

'Yes.'

'Nicole?'

'Yes.'

Leroy felt hope beginning to rise. Nicole. The name sounded familiar. Wasn't she . . .?

'Is Paulette there?' he asked in a rush.

'I think so,' said Veronica. 'Why?'

'I were lookin' fo' 'er.'

'Well, come an' see. It's only just up the road.'

As they walked along, Leroy told himself it was going to be all right. It wasn't definite yet, but there was a good chance. Paulette hadn't been kidnapped. She'd gone off to Nicole's birthday party.

Of course he could be wrong. But if she wasn't there, what had happened to her? Leroy didn't want to think about that.

'These bottles ain't 'alf 'eavy,' Veronica moaned.

Was she hinting?

Leroy struggled with himself and mumbled, ''Ere, I'll carry 'em.'

'Oh, Leroy,' Veronica gushed. 'Thank you.'

She handed the bag over. It seemed a small price to pay.

Veronica went on yapping. But Leroy didn't mind so much now. He didn't have to listen. He was thinking girls might have some use after all.

When they got to the house, they found that the party was coming to an end. Parents had arrived to take their children home. There was a crazy scramble as people searched for their coats and struggled into them.

Leroy spotted Paulette straightaway. He felt a great wave of relief. It was all right after all.

Then his mouth clamped tight shut. Wait till he got a hold of her!

Paulette caught sight of him and rushed over to him.

'Ooh, Leroy,' she cried, her eyes bright and her cheeks glowing. 'It were a great party.'

'Good,' said Leroy.

He would save the rest for later. When he had her alone.

There were shouts and laughs and goodbyes as people began to troop out of the house. Leroy heard Veronica cry, 'But what about this lemonade?' Nobody was listening to her.

As they hurried along, with Leroy dragging Paulette by the hand, she told him all about the party. Leroy heard it out with a grim face.

'It were good o' you to come an' fetch me,' she ended up saying.

'An' what if I 'adn't?' Leroy demanded.

'Ooh, I don' know,' Paulette said, her pleasure beginning to falter. 'I never t'ought o' that.'

'You'd 'ave 'ad to go 'ome on you' own, wouldn't you? An' you knows what Mum would say 'bout that.'

Paulette's face lost its smile. Her eyes became worried.

Leroy went on. 'An' why didn' you wait fo' me at school like you suppose?'

'I did wait,' Paulette defended herself. 'But you never come. An' they was all goin' off to Nicole's party so I t'ought it would be all right 'cause we was all goin' together.'

'Do Mum know 'bout the party?'

'No,' said Paulette. She bit her lip and her eyes grew watery. 'I forget to tell 'er.'

'Well, there gonna be a real row when you gets 'ome,' Leroy began.

Then he got into his stride.

'I been lookin' an' lookin' fo' you fo' hours. I didn' know where you was. I nearly go mad when I sees you ain't waitin' fo' me at school. I t'inks you been kidnapped or somet'in'. I were out my mind 'bout it.'

'Oh, Leroy,' Paulette whimpered. 'I'm sorry. Really I am.'

There were tears trickling down her cheek by now.

'Why don' you wipe you' face?' Leroy said gruffly and he waited while Paulette dried her tears and blew her nose.

Then he took her hand again and pressed on.

'We both gonna get lickin's when we gets 'ome 'less we can t'ink up some way out. Me fo' not meetin' you at school. An' you fo' goin' to that party on you' own wit'out tellin'.'

'Oh, Leroy,' Paulette pleaded. 'What we gonna do?'

Leroy thought about it.

'Well,' he said after a while, 'if you don' tell Mum I were late an' missed you, an' if I don' tell Mum you goes to that party on you' own, it might not be too bad.'

'But that's lyin',' Paulette protested.

'No, it ain't,' said Leroy.

He remembered what Mr Baxter had said about the school rule and not keeping him in when he was.

'It's a matter o' 'terpretation, that's all.'

Paulette didn't seem to understand.

Leroy explained. 'You can say to Mum you forgets to tell 'er 'bout the party, but I knew 'bout it. Well, I did. Eventually. Then I comes to make sure you gets 'ome all right. Well, I did, didn' I? All that's true. You just don' need to say not'in' 'bout all the other bits. There's still gonna be ructions, but maybe it won' be so bad.'

'All right,' said Paulette.

And that was what they did.

Mum was furious.

'I been worried sick. Two hours I been walkin' up an' down 'ere worryin' 'bout where you was. T'inkin' you was under a lorry or been mugged or somet'in'.'

Leroy was glad he hadn't thought of those possibilities.

'I were just 'bout to phone the police when you turns up.'

'But Mum,' Leroy argued. 'I knew Paulette were all right.'

Well, he did. In the end. But Mum wasn't having any of it.

'You!' she roared scornfully. 'Since when was you old enough to decide what to do? You ain't no man yet, an' don' you forget it.'

Leroy decided it was wiser to keep quiet and let the thunder roll over him.

'An' as fo' you, madam,' Mum went on, turning to Paulette, 'the next time you makes you' private arrangements, I wants to know 'bout 'em. An' if I don' know, you don' go. Understand?'

'Yes, Mum,' said Paulette with lowered eyes.

It could have been worse, Leroy thought later in the evening as he struggled with his maths homework. Mum went on rumbling, but the storm clouds were moving on. Luckily, Dad was on night shift. They'd be in bed long before he got home. He might have something to say about it in the morning, but the sting would have gone out of it by then.

Leroy congratulated himself. Yes, all in all, he'd got out of it rather well.

Then the point of his pencil broke as he pressed too hard on the page. He had suddenly remembered. It wasn't over yet.

There was tomorrow morning. He still had to face Mr **Baxter**.

Leroy's Prize-Giving

Mr Baxter was writing notes on the blackboard when there was a knock at the classroom door.

Leroy raised his head. His eyes widened. It was the headmistress, Mrs Worthington. It was the first time she had honoured their class with a visit during the three months they had been there.

Around him, Leroy heard the clatter of desks being pushed back and chair legs scraping the floor. The whole class jumped up.

Then he remembered. There was a rule about it, wasn't there? Number 87. Or was it Number 88? *When the headmistress enters a classroom, the pupils must stand up.*

Wearily Leroy hoisted himself off his seat.

Mr Baxter had been so absorbed in what he had been writing that he hadn't heard the knock. But he heard the thunder of moving furniture all right. He craned his head over his shoulder, alarmed that the class had risen in rebellion.

Then, when he saw Mrs Worthington, he became even more alarmed. He put his chalk down, rearranged his spectacles and nervously approached her.

But it was all right. Mrs Worthington was beaming at him and beaming at the pupils.

'Which class is this, Mr Baxter?' she asked cheerfully.

'It's 1B,' Mr Baxter told her.

'What a lovely class,' Mrs Worthington enthused. 'So keen. So attentive. So eager to learn.'

Then she seemed to notice for the first time that the pupils were all standing up.

'And so polite,' she added in impressed tones.

She made wild gestures in the air with her hands. She
might have been pushing the children away.

'Do sit down everyone,' she cried.

There was a shuffling and banging as the pupils resumed
their seats.

'Carry on with your work,' Mrs Worthington went on.
'Don't let me interrupt the lesson.'

Leroy pretended to concentrate on the notes on the blackboard, but out of the corner of his eye he watched Mrs
Worthington. He had seen her on the stage at assembly. He
had seen her having lunch in the dining room. But he had
never been as near to her as this before. He was surprised at
how small she was.

Mr Baxter seemed to be in a quandary. He didn't know
whether to continue writing up his notes or stop and be
polite to Mrs Worthington. The headmistress resolved the
dilemma herself. She began to talk to him confidentially.
Leroy strained to hear what she was saying. So did everyone
else.

'It's about the prize-giving tomorrow,' they heard. 'You
know the mayor and mayoress are coming.'

Mr Baxter nodded his head vigorously. Leroy thought it
would drop off if he wasn't careful.

'So kind and considerate of them,' Mrs Worthington went
on, 'especially when they're so busy. Engagements and
functions, day in, day out. And yet they find time for us. We
really do appreciate it.'

'Of course,' agreed Mr Baxter. 'It's marvellous. I don't
think they've been before, have they?'

Mrs Worthington didn't bother to answer Mr Baxter's
question. She didn't appear entirely to approve of it. She
hurried on.

'Anyway, we thought it would be only right that we
should present the mayoress with a bouquet.'

'Yes, yes,' agreed Mr Baxter, making amends. 'What a
good idea.'

'And I thought it would be nice if one of our new pupils

made the presentation. They're so fresh and eager. They haven't caught that dreadful adolescent apathy yet.' Mrs Worthington gave a kind of shudder, and her face screwed up with a sour look of distaste as though she'd just chewed on a lemon.

'I couldn't agree more,' said Mr Baxter.

Leroy sucked his teeth silently. Mr Baxter really was being very smarmy.

'So that's why I've come,' Mrs Worthington concluded. 'Can you suggest a suitable candidate?'

Mr Baxter went on smiling and nodding his head. Then he suddenly realized that Mrs Worthington had stopped talking and was expecting him to say something. He opened and shut his mouth a few times and went pink in the face.

'Yes,' he stammered. 'I'm sure we can find somebody.'

His gaze swept the class desperately before lighting on Veronica Wright.

Veronica knew he was looking at her. The whole class knew he was looking at her. She fluttered her eyelashes and opened her eyes wide and fixed them on Mr Baxter and Mrs Worthington. Butter wouldn't have melted in her mouth. Leroy felt like throwing up.

'Yes,' said Mr Baxter, 'I've got the very one. Veronica, stand up, please.'

With a great show of reluctance and embarrassment, Veronica squirmed in her seat and then drew herself up. It was like a snake uncoiling itself. The whole class stared at her.

Veronica fluttered her eyelashes again. It always worked with Mr Baxter.

But clearly not with Mrs Worthington.

'Oh no,' the headmistress cried immediately. 'I don't think that would be suitable at all.' She sounded most definite.

Veronica was shocked. Her face crumpled. She sank back into her chair, trying not to cry. Leroy tried to repress his feeling of glee.

'Gentlemen give flowers. It has to be a boy,' Mrs Worthington explained.

Quite right too, Leroy thought. Why should it always be girls who did things like that? Getting the limelight. Having the chance to show off. That was sexist, wasn't it? Mr Baxter was always going on about that.

It was suddenly very quiet. Leroy became aware of the silence. He squinted round. The whole class was looking at him. He turned to the front. Mrs Worthington was looking at him. A feeling of horror began to spread through him.

'What's your name?' Mrs Worthington was asking.

Leroy swallowed and told her.

'Oh yes,' Mrs Worthington cried. 'That's the one.'

Leroy heard a muffled splutter behind him. That was Calamity. Wait till he got him.

'D'you really think so?' Mr Baxter asked. His surprise must have got the better of him, daring to question her judgement like that.

'Of course,' said Mrs Worthington, examining him incredulously. 'He's perfect. That innocent face. Those round eyes. The bloom of childhood on his cheeks. And he's so big. The mayoress will be charmed. Nothing could be better.'

Leroy felt himself grow hot all over. He wanted to sink through the floor.

'If you say so,' Mr Baxter concurred. He studied Leroy for a moment before shaking his head in disbelief. Clearly he didn't see what Mrs Worthington was seeing.

Leroy couldn't see it either. He was outraged. Him presenting a bouquet! Him! A bouquet! He could hardly form the detested word in his mind. It wasn't right. That was something girls did. He'd never live it down.

But Mrs Worthington was oblivious of the ferment boiling inside Leroy.

'There's a rehearsal in the hall at break today,' she said. 'Mr Garfield's taking it. Make sure . . .'

She broke off and waved her hand in front of Leroy's face. 'What's your name again?'

'Leroy Brown,' Leroy muttered reluctantly.

'Of course, that's it,' Mrs Worthington said as though it was all Leroy's fault that she had forgotten.

She turned back to Mr Baxter. 'Make sure Leroy goes along. We want everything to go like clockwork. We don't want any mistakes in front of the mayor, do we?'

She gave Mr Baxter a grim smile and swept out of the room without waiting for a reply.

The class breathed a sigh of relief and broke into excited chatter. It was difficult having the headmistress there, having to be on one's best behaviour.

No one breathed a bigger sigh of relief than Mr Baxter. Then he pulled himself together. 'Get on with these notes then,' he barked at them, reasserting his authority. 'We've got a lot of work to get through.'

He pushed his spectacles up on his nose and peered at the blackboard to see how far he had got. He thought for a moment and then attacked the board frantically with his chalk.

Leroy was thinking too. What had he been let in for? Nobody had bothered to ask him if he wanted to present some rotten flowers. And he didn't.

'Psst,' came a hiss from behind.

Leroy inclined his head a mere inch in that direction and swivelled his eyes round in a brooding stare. He waited. He knew what was coming.

'Who's gonna give the mayoress some flowers then?' whispered Calamity. He sounded as if he were enjoying himself.

'Yeah,' Leroy growled back threateningly, 'an' who gonna get drill up?'

'Terence, get on with your work,' Mr Baxter snapped.

Serve him right, thought Leroy. He grudgingly returned to copying the notes from the board into his exercise book, but inside he went on fuming.

When the hooter sounded for break, Mr Baxter called him out to his desk.

'Now, remember what Mrs Worthington said,' he told him. 'You've to go to the hall and see Mr Garfield and rehearse for tomorrow. It's a great honour.'

'A great honour!' Leroy cried aghast. 'I don' want to present no flowers!'

'I can't help that,' said Mr Baxter. 'Mrs Worthington has decided.'

'But, sir!'

'No buts,' said Mr Baxter sternly.

Leroy turned on a top-voltage stare. The intensity was too much for Mr Baxter. He had to lower his eyes.

'Well it is an honour,' he insisted. But he didn't look up. 'Now don't let me down.'

Leroy knew it was useless to protest any more. He clamped his lips firmly together and stormed out of the classroom.

Calamity was waiting for him. He fell into a helpless heap of laughter when he saw Leroy. His knees gave way. He bent over double. His mouth was so wide Leroy hoped he would get lock-jaw.

'Who gonna give the mayoress flowers then?' Calamity squawked.

Leroy glared at him.

'Change the record,' he said.

It was meant to be cool, but he had the feeling he hadn't achieved quite the right tone.

It made no impression on Calamity's mirth.

Further along the corridor, Veronica Wright was moaning to her friend, Angie.

'It ain't fair. It ought to be me what's presentin' the bouquet.'

Her eyes sharpened into poisonous darts when she caught sight of Leroy.

'It's favouritism,' she snapped. 'That's what it is.'

Leroy pretended he hadn't heard. He went past with an exaggerated swagger that told the world he didn't care about anything Veronica Wright said.

But in a way he agreed with her. It wasn't fair. Why did it have to be him? There was such a thing as taking this equal-opportunity stuff too far.

And then there was his break. He would miss that as well.

He gave a resentful sigh. There was nothing he could do about it. The headmistress had picked him out and that was that.

In the hall, there was chaos. A boy was pretending to play the piano. Someone was opening and shutting the stage curtains. A gang of girls was chasing each other on and off the stage. Several boys had discovered they could slide on the polished floor.

Leroy watched them scornfully. He hadn't behaved like that even in his junior school. And these were the prize-winners!

Then Mr Garfield came marching into the hall roaring at the top of his voice.

'Shut that piano! Leave those curtains alone! Get off the stage! Stop that sliding!'

All activity miraculously ceased.

'Now,' Mr Garfield cried, 'I want two rows of chairs arranged along here.'

He jabbed out a finger and pointed. 'You, you and you, fetch some chairs from the back.'

Unwillingly, the three boys selected did what they were told. While the rest waited and watched, Mr Garfield grumbled at the reluctant chair-bearers, growing more and more irate.

'Lift them, don't slide them. I said two rows, not three. Can't you count? Don't you know what a straight line is? How you ever got the maths prize I'll never understand.'

Finally, after much clattering and shunting and banging about, the chairs were set out to Mr Garfield's satisfaction. He told them all to sit down.

There was a mad rush as people grabbed chairs, fought over them, plonked themselves down in them and refused to be budged.

Leroy didn't bother to try. It was like a game of musical chairs that had gone wrong.

He was the only first former there. The first year had only been at the school for three months, not long enough to get prizes.

But at least one mystery had been solved – why there were so many broken chair legs littering the corridors.

Then Mr Garfield noticed him.

'What do you want?' he barked.

Leroy explained about Mrs Worthington and the bouquet.

'I do wish someone would tell me these things,' Mr Garfield complained.

He gave an exasperated sigh. 'You'd better go and stand over there,' he told Leroy. 'I'll see to you later.'

Leroy felt even more left out as he leaned against the wall and watched Mr Garfield try to organize the pupils into the right order to get their prizes. Mr Garfield read out names from a typed list. As their names were called, pupils got up from their seats, clambered over the legs of others, ejected people from their chairs and took up their new positions. The displaced pupils stood about disconsolately.

'Sanjay Patel, Amrit Patel, Hitesh Patel,' Mr Garfield called out. 'Oh, do hurry up!'

'Sir, 'e won't let me past,' moaned a girl.

Mr Garfield glared at the boy who was blocking her way. The boy grinned back cheerfully.

'Oh, come along, Amrit. We haven't got all day.' He continued with his list. 'Kalpesh Patel, Nila Patel, Jane Smith.'

Somehow, with much squabbling and pushing and shifting about, the pupils ended up in the right order. Only Leroy remained standing at the side.

'Listen carefully. I don't want to have to go over this twice,' Mr Garfield said. He explained what they had to do. There were sets of steps leading from the floor of the hall to the stage at either side. The prize-winners had to go up one set of steps, walk to the centre of the stage, shake hands with the mayor, receive their prizes and come down the other set of steps. Meanwhile, everyone had to move one seat along so that there was an empty chair waiting ready at the end of the row for the prize-winner when he returned.

'We'd better run through it,' Mr Garfield said. 'I'll be the mayor.'

He climbed on to the stage. From the way the steps sagged under his weight, Leroy wondered whether they would survive that stream of traffic.

'Sanjay Patel,' Mr Garfield called out.

Sanjay got up, gave an embarrassed smirk and made for the steps. Immediately, the whole row stood up, and everyone moved one along. Chairs scraped along the floor. People pushed. Someone got shoved out of place. There were arguments.

'No, no, no!' yelled Mr Garfield. 'Not like elephants. Sit down. Do it again.'

This time, everyone moved with exaggerated stealth, shushing each other and walking on tiptoe. Mr Garfield seemed satisfied.

Sanjay continued up the steps, shook hands with Mr Garfield and came down on the other side. He seemed surprised to find there was actually a vacant chair waiting for him. Mr Garfield's plan apparently worked.

Leroy watched as, one after another, all the prize-winners went through the same performance. It became monotonous. Stand up, climb the steps, go to the centre, shake hands, walk off, sit down. Every time, there was a ghostly shuffling as the row moved along.

Then it was time for the second row to do the same.

It was taking hours. Break had finished ages ago. It was all right for them, Leroy thought. He heard some of them giggle with glee because they were missing French. But he had P.E. The rest of the class would be out on the field playing football by now.

First his break, and now P.E. It was too much.

But Mr Garfield hadn't finished yet. He went on to tell them how important prize-giving was. There would be lots of visitors and guests. They had to give a good impression.

'I want to see you all looking very smart,' he said. 'Full school uniform. Faces washed – and hands. Hair combed. Clean shirts. Ties done up. Shoes polished – and no trainers. And no earrings or jewellery. And that includes the boys. Is that understood?'

There were groans and murmurs of 'Yes, sir.'

'Right, you can go.'

There were more groans. 'Why couldn't he have kept us a bit longer?' someone complained. 'French hasn't finished yet.'

They ambled out of the hall, taking as long about it as they could, and leaving behind them a shamble of chairs and a litter of sweet wrappings.

Then there was just Leroy – and Mr Garfield.

The deputy head seemed surprised to see him.

'What do you want?' he demanded.

Leroy explained again about Mrs Worthington and the bouquet.

Mr Garfield groaned. 'Oh, yes.' It all came back to him. 'I wish you'd told me about it earlier,' he grumbled.

Leroy glowered, but he didn't dare say anything.

Mr Garfield went on complaining. 'I wish people would consult me. They put me in charge and then change the arrangements. I don't know.'

He ruminated on it for a while. 'When does one present a bouquet? At the end, I suppose. But other people might have different ideas.' He gave a contemptuous sniff. 'They usually do.'

Then he decided. 'You'd better sit on the first chair. That way we'll be ready for any eventuality. The secretary will have the bouquet, I suppose. You'd better collect it from the office and bring it down with you.'

He began to walk away.

Leroy went round-eyed with horror.

'But, sir,' he protested. 'You ain't told me what to do.'

Mr Garfield ground to a halt and turned round. 'What to do?' He sounded incredulous. 'But it's obvious, isn't it? You go up there, you give her the flowers, and you come down again. What's the problem?'

He didn't give Leroy time to tell him. He rounded on his heel and stalked stiffly but determinedly out of the hall.

Leroy could only stare after him. Well, that was a fat lot of use, wasn't it? It was bad enough having to present the bouquet in the first place. Now he would have to do it without a rehearsal, without quite knowing what he was supposed to do.

For the rest of the day, he had to put up with Veronica's sulks, and Calamity's jeers and taunts. But he survived. He was too anxious about what would happen next day to pay much attention to the jokes.

Even so it was a relief when the end of school came and he could get away from it all and go home.

But not for long.

Somehow or other, Floyd had heard all about it.

'Hey, Mum, guess what?' Floyd yelled as soon as he came in.

'Ain't no need to shout,' Mum admonished him. 'I ain't deaf.'

Floyd always spoke that way – as if he were at a football match.

'Leroy gonna present the bouquet at the prize-givin',' Floyd went on, trying to modulate his voice without much success. He gave a wild cackle. He seemed to think it was funny.

Leroy glowered at him.

'Oh?' said Mum. She thought about it and decided to approve. 'That's nice. I better make sure 'e got a clean shirt.'

Leroy groaned inwardly. There'd be no end to it now. She'd fuss and fuss.

She told Dad when he got home.

'What's flowers got to do wit' school?' Dad wanted to

know. 'Ain't 'e suppose to be gettin' a education? I don'
understand what schools is comin' to these days.'

He was in a bad mood. He wanted his dinner.

Later that evening, while Mum was ironing his shirt, she
said, 'I t'inks I goes along an' watch. They allows parents,
don' they, Leroy?'

'I don' know,' Leroy replied.

He didn't care either. It was getting worse and worse, and
there was nothing he could do about it.

He had a restless night. His mattress felt as though it were
filled with pebbles. He just couldn't get comfortable.
Through his head raced thoughts of the ordeal to come. Why
hadn't he refused to do it? Mrs Worthington couldn't have
done more than expel him for that. It would have been worth
it.

At breakfast next morning Paulette joined the band-
wagon.

'I wish I was at the big school,' she cried. 'I wanna see
Leroy give the lady the flowers.'

'Well, you can't,' growled Dad. 'Eat you' cornflakes.'

Mum wouldn't let Leroy out of the flat until she had
inspected him fully. She brushed a fleck of dust off the
shoulder of his blazer. She straightened and tightened his
tie. She held him firmly by the arms and slowly swung him
round while she examined every inch of his face.

'You sure you done you' ears?' she asked suspiciously.

'Course I did,' Leroy retorted indignantly.

'An' you' teeth?'

'Yeah.'

What was all this about? He was only handing over some
rotten flowers, not going to the dentist.

'All right,' said Mum at last. 'You'll do.'

Leroy was free to go.

'What time this t'ing suppose to be?' Mum asked.

''Alf past nine.'

'OK. I tries to be there.'

Leroy groaned. He thought Mum had changed her mind

about going. No such luck.

At school, you could sense the excitement. They had to stay in their form rooms until they were sent for to go down to the hall. They had to sit on their desks because all the chairs had gone. They'd been taken down to the hall already.

1B hadn't been to a prize-giving before. They were giggling and gossiping and buzzing with anticipation. Mr Baxter had difficulty maintaining order.

'Keep it down,' he warned, adjusting his spectacles and just managing to prevent a note of hysteria from creeping into his voice.

At a quarter past nine, he told Leroy he had better go to the hall. Leroy got up. He was sure every eye in the class followed him as he went out.

He remembered the instructions Mr Garfield had given him. He was to go to the office to collect the flowers and take them down to the hall.

The office was crowded. The secretary, Mrs Harris, was there of course, and her assistant, Miss Barnaby. But there were teachers as well. They were waving their hands about and talking excitedly. There was a sense of panic in the air.

Leroy examined the teachers more closely. There was something odd about them. Then he realized what it was. They were wearing gowns over their suits and dresses. Usually only Mrs Worthington and Mr Garfield wore gowns. Some of them were almost green with age. And they had strange things hanging down their backs. They were red and yellow and purple. Most of them were shiny, but one of them was furry. Leroy couldn't imagine what they were doing dolled up like that.

'What d'you want, love?' Mrs Harris asked at last, catching sight of him.

'The flowers,' Leroy told her.

'The flowers?' Mrs Harris's eyebrows went up an inch.

'The bouquet,' Leroy said.

'The bouquet?' Mrs Harris's eyebrows went up another inch.

'For the mayoress,' Leroy explained, getting desperate.

'For the mayoress?' Mrs Harris's eyebrows couldn't get any higher.

'Oh,' screeched Miss Barnaby. She must have been listening. 'It's not here yet.'

'What's not here?' asked Mrs Harris, mystified.

'The bouquet,' said Miss Barnaby.

'What bouquet?' demanded Mrs Harris.

At that moment, the connecting door to the headmistress's room opened, and Mrs Worthington came in. Perhaps she had been aroused by Miss Barnaby's screech.

'Everything all right?' Mrs Worthington asked as she beamed round at them all.

'Yes, yes,' said Mrs Harris hurriedly. 'No problems.'

'Good,' said Mrs Worthington. 'We want it all to go off smoothly.'

She gave another encouraging smile all round and returned to her room.

'What's all this about a bouquet?' Mrs Harris hissed at Miss Barnaby as soon as the door was shut.

'It was ordered yesterday,' Miss Barnaby replied, growing flustered. 'Mrs Worthington told me to do it. I forgot to tell you. Oh dear, what can have happened to it? They said they'd have it here by nine o'clock.'

'You'd better phone them,' said Mrs Harris, 'and find out what's keeping them.'

She turned to Leroy with a smile. 'Just hang on a minute, love. We'll sort it all out. Don't you worry.'

Leroy wasn't so confident. He had a sinking feeling in the pit of his stomach. It was all going wrong. And he was sure he would get the blame for it.

Miss Barnaby frantically dialled a number and listened intently.

'It's engaged,' she cried over her shoulder.

Mrs Harris's eyes swam upwards and disappeared. 'Isn't

that always the way? Well, if the worst comes to the worst, I can go down and collect it.'

She turned to Leroy again. Her face softened. 'It'll be all right, love, you'll see. Go down to the hall, and I'll bring the bouquet to you as soon as it arrives.'

As Leroy left the office, he heard her yelling, 'Well, ring them again!'

The hall was packed with chairs. The front row was practically on the stage, and they stretched line after line right to the back. They must have been taken from every classroom in the school. Along the edge of the stage there were pots of geraniums and ferns. It looked like a florist's shop. Leroy was glad he didn't suffer from hay fever.

The prize-winners had already arrived and were occupying the first two rows.

Leroy remembered what Mr Garfield had said. He was to sit in the first chair. But someone was already sitting there.

'I'm supposed to sit in that chair,' he told him.

The boy occupying the seat gave him a sullen glare. 'Get off,' he growled and went back to staring miserably into space.

Leroy was stumped. He didn't know what to do. Perhaps he could sit in the first seat of the third row of chairs, but that might upset other arrangements. Or should he just sit down cross-legged on the floor? That was what they usually did during Assembly. It was all such a mess that he felt like marching straight back to his form room.

Then Mr Garfield appeared.

'What are you doing here, boy?' he demanded sternly.

Leroy puffed out his cheeks. He held himself in. He explained again about the mayoress and the bouquet.

'Ah yes,' Mr Garfield said. 'Of course.'

Then he thought about it. Leroy could see his brain ticking over as memories from the past clicked into place. The fuse was being lit, the bomb was about to go off.

'I thought I told you to collect the bouquet from the office and bring it down. Where is it?' Mr Garfield blazed at him.

'It ain't 'ere yet,' Leroy told him.

'Well, it should be,' cried Mr Garfield, still blaming Leroy.

They glared at each other for a while. Mr Garfield seemed to be expecting Leroy to do something, though Leroy couldn't imagine what.

'I ain't got a seat,' Leroy said at last.

Mr Garfield groaned and raised his eyes to heaven.

He began waving his arms at the seated prize-winners and barking, 'Move along there.'

There was a shuffling of feet and a scraping of chairs and an undercurrent of grumbling as the prize-winners shifted over. The boy at the far end of the first row had to come and take the first chair of the second row.

Leroy sat down.

'That's all right then,' said Mr Garfield, and he breathed a sigh of relief.

''Ere, sir,' came a voice. 'I ain't got a seat.'

All heads turned. The boy at the end of the second row had nowhere to sit.

Mr Garfield went into a dance of fury. 'Get a chair from the back, you idiot,' he yelled.

'But I'll be sittin' in the gangway,' the boy protested.

Mr Garfield threw his arms into the air. 'Who cares?' he screamed.

Leroy lost interest after that. At least he was all right.

Gradually, the hall filled up. The form teachers brought their classes down and settled them into their places. A subdued murmuring flowed throughout the hall. But it wasn't in any way excessive. The school knew how to behave when there were visitors about.

Mr Garfield stood on the stage and held them all with a baleful eye. Teachers walked up and down the aisles, swishing their gowns. Mr Baxter didn't have one, Leroy noticed. He wondered why.

He took a quick look behind him. 1B was sitting immediately behind the prize-winners. Leroy caught Calamity's inane grin and Veronica's sour scowl. He gazed beyond them at the rest of the school, seated rank upon rank. At the very back, there were adults being shown to their seats. They must have been parents. He couldn't see Mum.

He turned to the front again and began to worry. What was he supposed to do? Nobody had brought the bouquet yet. He could imagine the whole scene. Mrs Worthington would proclaim, 'And now I call upon Leroy Brown to present a bouquet to the mayoress,' and there he would be – empty-handed. He shuddered at the very thought.

There was a sudden hush. Mr Garfield swelled himself up to his fullest height and cried, 'Stand up!'

While the whole school rose to its feet, a procession of dignataries led by the headmistress made its way down the aisle. Leroy watched as they staggered up the steps on to the stage. They were all so ancient. He wondered if they would survive the ceremony.

There was a great deal of confusion on the stage as they sorted out where they were going to sit. The school remained standing patiently while they found their places. Then Mr Garfield shouted, 'Sit down!' and everyone subsided into their seats.

There was an expectant silence.

Mrs Worthington began to look apprehensive. She leaned over to the man on her right and whispered something.

'What?' the man cried, startled. 'Oh!'

He cranked himself to his feet. He adjusted his face into a beneficent smile.

'Good morning, children,' he said.

There was no response.

He cupped his hand to his ear and said, 'What? I didn't hear you. Good morning.'

Half-heartedly, the pupils moaned back, 'Good morning, sir.'

The man grunted. 'Ah! That's better.'

Then he went on. 'I had better introduce myself. My name is Marks. I am your Chairman of Governors. And it's a great pleasure for me to be here this morning at your annual prize-giving. I remember when I was at school how much I looked forward to prize-giving. Of course, that was a very long time ago. And I never won a prize.'

He broke off into a dry cackle and then fell into a coughing fit. But no one else laughed.

He smothered his nose and mouth with his handkerchief, had a good spit, and then continued. 'But that wasn't the point . . .'

He went on and on. Leroy stopped listening. He surreptitiously turned and looked up the aisle. There was no sign of Mrs Harris.

'And so that is why I enjoy prize-giving,' Mr Marks concluded.

He began to sit down and then remembered that he hadn't quite finished.

'Oh,' he said, straightening up as far as he was able, 'I ought to introduce the rest of the platform to you. We are very honoured to have his worshipful the mayor, Councillor Lewis, with us today as our guest of honour to present the prizes.'

Councillor Lewis leaned forward and nodded his grinning head at the assembled pupils.

'And with him of course,' Mr Marks continued, 'his delightful mayoress, Mrs Lewis. We are very pleased to have you here, ma'am.'

Mrs Lewis bared her teeth in a gracious smile.

Mr Marks looked left and right at the people on the stage, and seemed at a loss as to whom to introduce next. Mrs Worthington hurriedly consulted with him.

'Ah yes,' Mr Marks cried, recovering himself. 'I'm sure you all know the person on my left – your headmistress, Mrs Warrington.'

Mrs Worthington hissed at him.

'What?'

Mrs Worthington repeated herself.

'Yes, that's right,' said Mr Marks. 'Mrs Worthington.'

He went on to introduce the other governors and guests with several promptings from the headmistress.

Leroy took another quick look round. Everyone seemed to be asleep. He couldn't see Mrs Harris.

Mr Marks appeared to have finished. He attempted to sink back into his seat. But before he could do so, Mrs Worthington whispered something to him.

'What?' he demanded.

Mrs Worthington went on whispering. Mr Marks held the table in front of him with his hands and pulled himself up.

'And now I call on your headmistress, Mrs Warrington, to give her annual report.'

Mrs Worthington gave Mr Marks a sharp glance and rose to her feet.

'Thank you, Mr Chairman,' she said icily.

Then she thawed and filled the whole hall with her smile.

'It's so lovely to welcome you all here – pupils, old pupils, parents, governors, guests. We like to think of our prize-giving as a family occasion, a chance for us all to be together to honour those pupils who have worked hard and achieved something of value.'

She paused for a moment's thought and then launched out again.

'We had a splendid year last year . . .'

She went on and on. Floyd told Leroy later that she said the same thing every year. There were lists of examination successes, sports records broken, university places gained, charities supported, extra-mural activities undertaken. By the end, Leroy felt as though he had been flattened into his seat, smothered by information, battered by statistics.

But at last she had finished. She sat down.

There was a hiatus while nothing happened.

Then Mrs Worthington began giving urgent messages to the Chairman.

'What?' Mr Marks squawked.

Mrs Worthington persisted.

Mr Marks groaned and dragged himself to his feet.

'Thank you, Mrs Warrington,' he said, nodding in the direction of the headmistress. 'I'm sure we are all most gratified by what you and your staff are doing for the school.'

He turned and smiled down at the prize-winners. There was an awkward pause. He seemed to have forgotten what to do next.

Mrs Worthington repeated her instructions.

'Ah, yes,' said Mr Marks. 'It gives me great pleasure to call upon his worshipful the mayor, Councillor Lewis, to present the prizes.'

He fell back into his chair, exhausted.

The mayor stood up and stepped forward, smiling ingratiatingly around the assembly.

Mr Garfield stood up and stepped forward too. He called out the first name.

There was applause from the hall. The boy sitting next to Leroy – Sanjay – stood up. He frowned furiously at Leroy for a moment and then climbed over Leroy's outstretched legs. He nearly went sprawling on to the floor, but he recovered his balance in time to go bounding up the steps to get his prize.

The whole row rose and shifted along.

''Ow come you so big?' the girl who was now sitting next to Leroy whispered.

'I can' 'elp it,' Leroy defended himself.

''Ow the 'eck am I gonna get past you? Stick your legs in the aisle.'

Leroy did as he was told. As he did so, he noticed that there was a man with a camera standing there leaning against the wall. It must have been someone from the local newspaper.

It was agony sitting like that, but the girl managed to squeeze past when her name was called. The row shifted along again.

Leroy soon grew tired of sitting in that awkward position. He also grew tired of the dirty looks he got from each new occupant of the seat next to him. It was quite a relief to find

Sanjay sitting beside him once more as they started on the second row. He could bring his legs back to normal.

One thing though. It had taken his mind off his big worry for at least five minutes. But now it all came surging back again. Where was that bouquet? It would soon be time, wouldn't it? Leroy squinted round, but there was still no sign of Mrs Harris. What was he going to do?

All the prizes had been given out by now, and the mayor was informing them that he would like to say a few words to them. Though his idea of 'a few' seemed rather odd to Leroy.

He got the general drift of what the mayor said. The mayor had never got any prizes at school. (Hadn't Mr Marks said that as well?) He'd been a naughty boy. But that hadn't stopped him. Look at him now. He was the mayor. So there was hope for all naughty boys. And naughty girls, he hastily added. They could all become mayors. Or mayoresses.

Leroy couldn't see the point of it all. He didn't want to become mayor.

But then, after quarter of an hour, it looked as though the mayor was drawing to a close. Leroy suddenly wanted him to go on for ever. The awful moment was almost upon him. He would be exposed for what he was – a fraud – sitting in the front row with no right, with nothing to present.

The mayor sat down and was applauded. Mrs Worthington urged Mr Marks to his feet again and hissed something in his ear. It had to be now. Leroy wished the earth would open and swallow him up.

But before Mr Marks could get any words out, there was a tapping at the back of the hall. Mr Marks stared transfixed. All eyes turned and necks craned to see what it was. Leroy swung round too.

It was Mrs Harris. She was walking carefully down the aisle, placing one foot in front of the other and swaying from side to side as she tried without much success to prevent her high heels from clicking on the parquet floor. In her arms was a huge bouquet.

Leroy had never been so glad to see anyone before in his whole life.

It seemed to take an eternity for her to reach him. She was taking such small steps. But at last she arrived and deposited the bouquet on Leroy's lap. He had a quick glimpse of her face. It was burning.

Then, still taking tiny steps, putting one foot in front of the other, and swaying from side to side, she went back up the aisle.

Everyone watched. In total silence. Fascinated.

Even after she had gone, Mr Marks went on staring. Mrs Worthington had to nudge him.

'Ah yes,' he said coming back to earth. Leroy listened intently. 'I have one final duty to perform, and it is a very pleasant one. It is only fitting that we should show our appreciation to the mayoress for gracing our platform this morning. I therefore ask . . . ask . . . ask . . .'

He sounded like a record that had got stuck. Mrs Worthington was trying to convey some message to him, but he couldn't make out what it was. He just went on.

'. . . the boy in the front row to present her with a bouquet.'

This was it. Leroy took a deep breath and got up. It would soon be over.

But worse was to come. He climbed the steps and held the bouquet out to the mayoress. It was enormous, flowers of every colour and shape sealed in cellophane.

Then the mayoress took over. She raised her hands in surprise and her face lit up with delight.

'Oh,' she enthused. 'Isn't that lovely?'

She accepted the bouquet and cradled it expertly in one arm. Then she smiled at Leroy.

'Such a sweet boy,' she said. 'You deserve a reward.'

The people in the hall were clapping so they didn't hear what the mayoress said, but they saw what she did all right. She leaned forward, drew Leroy towards her with her free hand and planted a resounding kiss on his cheek.

At the same time, there was a flash as the press photographer took a photograph. And a chorus of oohs and aahs swept over the hall.

Leroy was mortified. He knew he was blushing. He would never be able to live it down.

As if that wasn't enough, he had another shock when he staggered down the steps to his seat. It had gone. While he had been on the stage, the whole row had shifted along.

Leroy glared at Sanjay and the others, but they just smiled innocently back at him. All he could do was stand there and wait.

The platform party was getting ready to leave. Mr Marks was having a final word.

'And I hope you all have a happy Easter,' he said.

Mrs Worthington muttered something to him.

Leroy heard the words 'Happy Christmas'.

'What?' queried Mr Marks. 'Oh, thank you. And the same to you.'

'No, no,' cried Mrs Worthington, and she went on muttering.

'Ah, yes,' cried Mr Marks. 'Thank you, Mrs Warrington.' He turned to the pupils again. 'I mean have a happy Christmas.'

Mr Garfield stepped forward and called the pupils to attention. One by one, the guests struggled down the steps and straggled up the aisle out of the hall.

Then, before Mr Garfield could tell them what to do next, Mrs Worthington was back. Leroy was surprised to see her at his elbow. She was speaking to him.

'When you're dismissed, come to the library, Leroy,' she said. 'The mayoress wants you to join us for refreshments.'

She was smiling, but the smile had a strained edge to it. Leroy had a feeling she was put out.

He was bewildered too. What was he going to do mixing with all those guests? The idea of 'refreshments' sounded all right, though.

The pupils left the hall row by row, starting at the back, so

Leroy was the last to get out.

Some of the parents were still in the foyer, chatting to each other. Leroy saw Mum. And Dad was there too, in his bus driver's uniform. He must have got time off or swapped his shift. They came over to him.

'You done that real well,' said Mum. She was smiling proudly.

'An' you gets you' picture in the paper too,' said Dad with a big grin. 'That's real somet'in'.'

Leroy wasn't so sure. It was bad enough the whole school seeing the mayoress kiss him. Now everyone on the estate would see it as well.

'I gotta go to the library fo' refreshments,' Leroy told his parents. He tried to make it sound casual and important at the same time.

'Well then,' said Mum, impressed. 'You mind you' manners.'

'Yeah, yeah,' Leroy said impatiently. Why did she have to keep reminding him of things like that?

Outside the library, Leroy waited for a moment to summon up enough courage to knock. He went in. The first thing he saw were the tables. They had been rearranged. The scratched graffiti-engrained surfaces were hidden by table-cloths. And laid out on them was plate after plate of food. Leroy's eyes darted from one to another in a rapid inventory – sausage rolls, mince pies, jam tarts, meringues, peanuts, crisps, sticks with cheese and ham on them, more sticks with cheese and pineapple, sandwiches, biscuits. He was amazed by the sight of so much.

The guests were already there, chatting and laughing. The mayoress came forward to welcome him. For a moment, Leroy thought she was going to kiss him again.

'Well, if it isn't my little Rosenkavalier,' she laughed.

Leroy didn't know what she was talking about.

But he didn't have to answer. The mayoress just breezed on. 'I thought it was only fair you should join us for this lovely beanfeast after you presented the flowers so beautifully. I insisted.' She turned to the headmistress who was standing beside her. 'Didn't I?'

Mrs Worthington managed an icy smile.

'Now you go and help yourself,' the mayoress continued to Leroy. 'Tuck in. It'll make you grow.'

Leroy didn't wait for a second telling. As he picked up a plate and wondered what to try first, he heard the mayoress say to Mrs Worthington, 'He *is* big for a first former, isn't he?'

A lot of the teachers were coming in now. Trust them not to miss a free meal, Leroy thought, as he stuffed a sausage roll into his mouth.

Mr Baxter was there. 'You did that very nicely, Leroy,' he said. He sounded surprised.

There was coffee to drink, and orange squash and sherry. So that was what happened to the school fund, thought Leroy. He picked up a glass of orange at the same time as Mr Garfield grabbed a glass of sherry. The way the deputy head gulped it down, it might just as well have been orange squash.

A lot of the people talked to Leroy. They asked him how old he was, and what his favourite subjects were, and what he wanted to be when he grew up, and things like that. But mostly, they talked to each other. Leroy didn't mind. He couldn't talk and eat at the same time.

As he moved round the tables, deciding what to eat next, he heard odd scraps of conversation.

'It's quite a spread,' one teacher said to another. 'The kitchen ladies have done us proud.'

'It's only because the Chief Education Officer's here,' retorted his colleague. 'We'll be on short rations for the next month, I bet. Thick mince and mash.' He picked up another jam tart.

'I can't think why I said Easter instead of Christmas,' Mr Marks was saying to the mayor. 'Perhaps time just goes faster when you're old.'

Mrs Worthington was looking daggers at Mr Garfield.

'How would he like it,' she hissed, 'if I went around calling him Mr Spencer?'

Mr Garfield emptied the contents of his glass and searched around for a replacement.

Mrs Harris was in earnest conference with Miss Barnaby. 'I was so embarrassed,' she was saying. Then she sniffed. 'I tell you, the next time she wants flowers, she can go and get them herself,' she said emphatically.

'Quite right,' agreed Miss Barnaby, being supportive. They helped themselves to more sandwiches.

People began to leave. Leroy thought he had better go as well. He didn't want to outstay his welcome. But how? The mayoress was busy talking to Mrs Harris. The headmistress was lecturing the mayor about something. Mr Garfield was smiling and staring into space, lost in a world of his own.

So he just had a final meringue and walked out.

It was still break. Leroy went up to the top playground and was surprised to find himself surrounded by a horde of girls. He looked round him for a way of escape and tried to draw back.

'That were lovely,' cried Marie, 'the way you give 'er the flowers.'

'Yeah,' said Lorraine. 'An' the way she kissed you.'

Veronica was there too. 'It ain't fair,' she moaned. 'It should 'ave been me what 'ad my picture in the paper.'

'Yeah,' said Lorraine, 'but she wouldn't 'ave kissed you, would she?'

'That's just sexist then,' Veronica protested.

But nobody was interested in what she said. They were all gazing at Leroy with awe and admiration.

'I'm gonna ask my dad to get a copy of the paper,' said Marie.

'Yeah,' said Lorraine. 'I'm gonna cut your picture out.'

'Me too,' said Stephanie. 'Will you autograph it for me?'

She waited with bated breath for Leroy's reply.

He examined her coolly and pursed his lips. 'I t'inks 'bout it,' he said and strolled away.

But he was thinking that perhaps it wasn't so bad after all being kissed by the mayoress.

There was a yell from behind, and Calamity came charging up to him.

'Where you been?' he demanded suspiciously.

Leroy turned a disdainful glance on him. 'I been 'avin' refreshments,' he told him. 'Wit' the guests.' It sounded very grand. Leroy enjoyed the look, a mixture of disbelief and envy, that flooded Calamity's face.

'I 'ad three sausage rolls,' Leroy went on.

'You what?' cried Calamity.

'An' four mince pies.'

''Ow many?'

'Two meringues. Four jam tarts. Three sticks wit' cheese an' 'am, an' two wit' cheese an' pineapple. Three sandwiches — salmon I t'inks they was. I lost count o' 'ow many peanuts an' crisps I 'ad.'

Calamity was staring at him and gasping. His tongue came out and rapidly licked his lips. He swallowed.

'Oh yeah,' Leroy went on, suddenly remembering, 'an' four glasses o' orange squash.'

Calamity was lost for words. He just stood there and gawped.

Leroy felt quite pleased with himself. It hadn't turned out so badly after all. He wouldn't mind now if they asked him to present a bouquet next year.

He might even volunteer.